History of
THE SOMERSET LIGHT INFANTRY
1946 – 1960

Field-Marshal The Lord Harding of Petherton, G.C.B.,
C.B.E., D.S.O., M.C. Colonel of the Regiment

History of
THE SOMERSET
LIGHT INFANTRY

(PRINCE ALBERT'S)

1946 – 1960

by

KENNETH WHITEHEAD

with a foreword by

FIELD-MARSHAL THE LORD HARDING OF PETHERTON
G.C.B., C.B.E., D.S.O., M.C.

Colonel of the Regiment

Maps drawn by
CAPTAIN J. F. A. OVERTON

Published by
THE SOMERSET LIGHT INFANTRY

CONTENTS

Contents

Contents

FOREWORD

by

FIELD-MARSHAL LORD HARDING

THIS is the final volume of the history of the Somerset Light Infantry as a Regular Regiment of the British Army. It covers the period between 1946 and 1960: the aftermath of the Second World War; the withdrawal from India; service in Greece, Austria and Germany; operations in the jungles and swamps of Malaya; mobilization for the abortive Suez operations; demonstrations for the School of Infantry at Warminster; and finally amalgamation with The Duke of Cornwall's Light Infantry—the birth of a new Regiment with all the fame and glory of the old.

It is a proud story of devoted and distinguished service in many different parts of the world in the best traditions that the Regiment maintained throughout its long life of two hundred and seventy-four years; a record of which all who helped to make it can feel and know that they worthily upheld the great name and reputation established by their forebears.

Major Whitehead has told the story faithfully and well. Having served with the 1st Battalion in Malaya, he writes with first-hand knowledge of the operations there. It was particularly fortunate that he was ready to undertake the work, and the Regiment owes him a great debt of gratitude for the way he has carried out the task.

To every reader I would say: Remember!—Remember that the courage and devotion, the self-sacrifice and comradeship, the spirit of the men who walk these pages, lives on. Their story, their exploits, their endeavours will be a never-failing source of strength and courage to the future generations that succeed them in the Somerset and Cornwall Light Infantry. Of that I am convinced. That is their pride and their reward.

Harding of Petherton

F.M.

20 July 1960

PREFACE

EVERY subaltern hopes that he will one day command a regular battalion of his Regiment. That has not been my fortune; but I take it as a high honour and some recompense, that to me should have fallen the task of writing the final volume of the Regimental History.

For the Infantryman the period has been no easy one: the uneasy aftermath of war; the Cold War; Malaya; Suez; the multitude of onerous and honourable peace-time duties— an unbalanced period which is reflected in the description of events and makes for uneven recording. The reader must not therefore be surprised to find that the major part of the book deals with three years in Malaya.

To relate these three years presents many problems, and although I have striven to adhere to the chronological order of events, I have not allowed this to mar the unfolding of the tale. I have occasionally simplified disjointed events in the interests of coherence—those who were in Malaya will remember that events were rarely at the time coherent. Nor, in the interests of readability, have I mentioned every single incident. For this I make no excuse.

I have seen fit to include an opening chapter recapitulating the history of the Regiment up to 1946. This is intended for those who may be unable to acquire the earlier volumes which are now out of print, and thus this final volume contains, however inadequately, the complete history of the Regiment. I have also included a brief history of the Duke of Cornwall's Light Infantry, and their affiliated South African Regiment, for the benefit of those members of the Regiment who are now members of the Somerset and Cornwall Light Infantry. There are also short accounts of the histories of the Royal Hamilton Light Infantry and the Macquarie Regiment.

I owe a great debt to the Regimental History Committee, particularly Colonels Hunt and Urwick at Taunton, for their patience, help and co-operation. Brigadiers Howard and Brind and Colonel Baily have also given me advice and furnished valuable material. No one writing this history could have done so without the *Light Bob Gazette*; it has been the basic material from which I have worked: in particular the contributions by Colonel C. C. A. Carfrae and Major D. J. R. Parker have been invaluable both for content and style. The other main source has been the War Diaries kept by a succession of Intelligence Officers of the 1st Battalion, and I am greatly indebted to Captains D. R. Goddard and D. A. Forbes, Lieutenant D. Hancock and Mr J. H. F. Mackie for their accurate and colourful reports. In addition I am most grateful to Captain C. D. C. Frith, Captain D. R. Goddard, Captain D. T. L. Beath and Mr E. D. Capper for providing material for certain events and facts. Brigadier J. R. I. Platt and Major T. L. Ingram have also given me background information and help. Colonels W. Q. Roberts, C. J. Stewart, E. A. Trotman and T. H. Harding have given me important details concerning the Territorials. Without the phenomenal memory of Mr Holt at the Depot, I would have been hard put to it when preparing some of the appendixes. Mr Clark of the 1st Battalion Orderly Room has also helped me with certain basic facts. Finally, not only am I, but so is the whole Regiment, indebted to Major J. J. Ogilvie, of William Clowes & Sons, Ltd., for seeing the history through their press.

London,   K.J.W.
30 December 1960

Acknowledgement

The Regiment is greatly indebted to the late ex-Colour Sergeant Frederick John Bindon of the Regiment, whose generosity has made funds available to assist in the publication of this history.

ILLUSTRATIONS

Illustrations

MAPS

CHAPTER ONE

A HERITAGE

A Summary of the History of the Regiment 1685–1945

WHAT is the Regiment? A name? A history? A badge? Men? A style of drill? A uniform? All these things and something more, for these are not sufficient in themselves. Indeed the XIIIth has had many names; its history has grown day by day; the badge has changed. Men have come and gone; drill has varied with the weapons; uniforms have altered with fashion. But the Regiment has always been there: changeable but solid and, even when changing, permanent.

From Huntingdon's Foot has run a magic solvent which, through two hundred and seventy-four years of change and variation has worked so as to ensure that the Regiment has maintained a certain way of life, a standard of service and an ethos of its own. What this magic solvent may be, unless it be tradition, no man can tell for sure. But on 12 September 1959 the handiwork of this magic could be seen when the men of the 1st Battalion The Somerset Light Infantry and the assembled ex-members of the Regiment paraded together for the last time and could be seen to be moved, one and all, from the youngest recruit to the oldest veteran, by the same invisible force.

After the troubles of the Civil War and the rude rule of Cromwell's major-generals, the nation was heartily sick of soldiers. Charles II had therefore to content himself with no more than a nominal military force. James II, a more military and autocratic personality, not content with this, strengthened the Crown by raising additional regiments. Amongst those authorized to raise a regiment of foot was Theophilus, 7th Earl of Huntingdon, who did so in the year 1685. It was granted precedence as the XIIIth Regiment of Foot, which proud and distinctive number it has held ever since. In due course, and after many changes, this Regiment became the Somerset Light Infantry (Prince Albert's).

After the deposition and flight of James II the army transferred its allegiance to William of Orange, and the young Regiment was sent to deal with various insurrections in support of the dethroned monarch. Its first battle was the disastrous defeat at Killiecrankie where, alone of King William's troops, it withstood unbroken the charging Highlanders. Later it went to Ireland and fought at the Battle of the Boyne and at the capture of Cork and Kinsale. With a Dutch King on the throne, committed to a European war against the ambitions of Louis XIV, it was not long before England became engaged on the Continent. In 1701, under Marlborough, the Regiment had its first experience of fighting in the Low Countries, being engaged at Nijmegen, Venlo and Liège. In 1703 it took part in the siege and capture of Huy.

The War of the Spanish Succession involved the whole of Europe, and the Regiment was part of the expedition which relieved the besieged fortress of Gibraltar and then remained to help to defend the fortress for the remainder of the eight-month siege. During the siege, under Colonel Moncal, they took a prominent part in repulsing the only dangerous enemy attack. This was the first Battle Honour to be borne on the Colours.

In 1704 the Regiment joined Lord Peterborough's force that captured Barcelona. This versatile general, wishing to have a larger number of cavalry for the more mobile prosecution of the campaign, converted the Regiment into Dragoons under the command of Lieutenant-Colonel Pearce—hence the name 'Pearce's Dragoons'—and as such it took part in the capture of Valencia and the remainder of this campaign. Meanwhile Lord Barrymore, the Colonel of the XIIIth, returned to England to re-raise his regiment of foot and in due course returned to Portugal with it, campaigning there until the peace in 1710. Leaving Portugal, the Regiment went as garrison to Gibraltar, where it still was in 1727 when the Spaniards again besieged the fortress for six months.

During the War of the Austrian Succession the Regiment went to Europe and, under the command of King George II himself, fought at the Battle of Dettingen—the second Battle Honour—and in 1745 in the heroic and costly attack at Fontenoy. The Highlanders meanwhile rising under the Young Pretender, the Regiment was hurried home to take a distinguished part in the Battle of Culloden. Lord Mark Kerr claimed that from this battle dated the sergeant's distinction of wearing their sashes over the right shoulder. Once the rising had been quelled, the Regiment returned to the Continent and fought at the Battle of Lauffeld.

As a result of new ideals born of the French Revolution, the Caribbean natives, supported by the French, rose in rebellion and an expedition was sent to protect British interests. In 1793 the XIIIth Somersetshire Regiment—for the Regiment was now connected with the County—took part in a series of difficult minor operations on the island of San Domingo. Disease, however, was more deadly than the enemy and the Regiment was soon reduced to a pathetically weak condition.

In 1800 the Regiment joined General Abercrombie's force which, after a few abortive operations on the coast of Spain, carried out the brilliantly successful assault-landing on the beaches of Aboukir Bay in Egypt. They then advanced on Alexandria, where Napoleon's garrison capitulated. The Sphinx and the word 'Egypt' on the Colours commemorate this campaign.[1]

From 1808 until 1810 the Regiment was again in the Caribbean, taking part in the capture of the islands of Guadeloupe

---

[1] The assault-landing at Aboukir Bay is not only one of the first assault-landings, but also one of the first combined operations carried out by the Royal Navy and the Army. On this occasion General Abercrombie ensured success by meticulous rehearsals in the Greek islands near by; rehearsals that might well have changed the outcome in the Dardanelles, as they did so amply in Normandy.

and Martinique from the French. 'Martinique' became the third Battle Honour. As the war widened, the Americans invaded Canada and the Regiment was sent to help the settlers, thus gaining its first experience of frontier warfare and learning the value of light infantry tactics in the forests. Although hurried home to help in the campaign caused by Napoleon's escape from Elba, it arrived too late for Waterloo.

In 1823 the XIIIth Somersetshire Light Infantry—for the Regiment had recently been converted to Light Infantry— landed at Calcutta for its first tour in the East. Almost at once it was engaged in the First Burmese War, fighting in the appallingly difficult river and jungle terrain and winning the Battle Honour 'Ava'.

In 1839 the Regiment was part of the column that invaded Afghanistan, crossing the Bolan Pass, taking Ghazni by storm and capturing Kandahar and Kabul. Once matters in Kabul seemed settled, General Sale's Brigade, which included his own regiment the XIIIth, was ordered back to India.[1] There was trouble at once with the tribesmen and the force had to fight its way through the passes. On reaching the little fort of Jellalabad they were besieged by the Afghans. Meanwhile, the main army, also trying to regain India, was attacked in the passes and destroyed with the exception of one man, the gallant Doctor Brydon, *Remnants of an Army*. The siege dragged on: the garrison made two sorties: they repaired the walls knocked down by earthquakes. Not the least of their anxieties was the fate of their womenfolk, Lady Sale amongst them, who were in Afghan hands.[2] The final sortie was made on 7 April 1842 led by General Sale, Colonel Dennie and

[1] General Sir Robert Sale was the first outstanding soldier produced by the Regiment. He was later, fighting characteristically in the forefront of the battle, severely wounded at the Battle of Mudkee in the Sikh War and died of his wounds.

[2] Lady Sale was a quite exceptional woman. Her account of the negotiations in Kabul before the army's disastrous retreat is of great interest as are also her adventures when in Afghan hands. Details of this remarkable book are in the Bibliography.

4

Captain Havelock[1] and was completely successful. The vast Afghan force was utterly routed. Later the heroic Lady Sale and her party of women and wounded were rescued from their captors. Honours showered on the Regiment; Queen Victoria approved the addition of the words 'Prince Albert's' to the title; the Regimental facings were changed from their original yellow to royal blue; the mural crown and title 'Jellalabad' was added to its appointments; a special medal was struck. Later, when the Indian Government avenged the disaster in Afghanistan, the Regiment was part of the punitive column that again entered Kabul and erased the defeat. It is notable that the Regiment, though never designated Royal, from then on had the distinctions normally associated with that title.

The Regiment and its comrades of the siege, the 35th Bengal Native Infantry and a party of Sappers, were accorded a triumphal march through India on their return. The XIIIth and the 35th arranged reciprocal entertainments, exchanging hospitality and gifts. The soldiers of the XIIIth presented their native comrades with the interesting piece of silver, the Attar-dan, which, as the 35th was disbanded during the Mutiny, has only recently been re-discovered and is now in the museum at Sandhurst. Three Battle Honours were awarded for this campaign: 'Ghuznee, 1839', 'Affghanistan, 1839' and 'Cabool, 1842'.

In 1855 the Regiment was sent to the Crimea, arriving in time to take part in the final stages of the siege of Sevastopol: the eighth Battle Honour. In 1857 the Regiment was hurried to India to assist in quelling the Mutiny. Under Lord Mark Kerr it fought a sharp engagement at Azimghur. Sergeant William Napier and Private Patrick Carlin both won Victoria Crosses: the first to be won by members of the Regiment.

[1] Henry Havelock, who later commanded the Regiment, became a national figure during the Indian Mutiny. By this time a general, he led the first column to the relief of the Duke of Cornwall's Light Infantry besieged at Lucknow. He was not only a great leader but a particularly noble and saintly man.

A Heritage

In 1878–9 the 1st Battalion—for the 2nd Battalion had been raised at Winchester in 1858—was in South Africa. It was engaged in fighting the Kaffir chieftain Sekukini and the formidable Zulu warrior-leader Cetewayo. Fighting the Zulus, Major W. Knox-Leat won the Victoria Cross. The Battle Honour 'South Africa, 1878–9' was awarded for this campaign, fought against the pride of the Zulu impis.

The 2nd Battalion had their first active service in 1885, in the Second Burmese War. This resolved itself into minor actions by subordinate commanders amongst the stockades, swamps and jungle rivers in most unpleasant conditions. The Battle Honour 'Burma, 1885–87' was added to the Colours after this war. In 1897 the 1st Battalion was engaged on the North-west Frontier of India fighting Pathans and Afghans in the Momand campaign. The 2nd Battalion took part in the South African War, being in the force that relieved Ladysmith—another Battle Honour—and then was engaged in many other battles with the Boers. The twelfth Battle Honour, 'South Africa 1889–1902', was awarded at the end of this long drawn-out war.

On the outbreak of the First World War the 1st Battalion was in England, a part of the Expeditionary Force; the 2nd Battalion was in India. From the very first moments of the war the 1st Battalion was engaged, and fought in the retreat from Mons and at the Battles of the Marne and Aisne. They suffered heavy casualties. The 2nd Battalion spent the whole war in India until, in 1919, they took part in the Third Afghan War, winning the Battle Honour 'Afghanistan, 1919'. Initially, most of the Territorial Force battalions were sent to India. From there the 1st/4th Battalion went to Mesopotamia; they took part in the unsuccessful attempt to relieve the ill-fated garrison of Kut-el-Amara and later went on to capture Baghdad. The 2nd/4th and 1st/5th joined General Allenby's army which captured Ghaza and Jerusalem. In addition to the Regular and Territorial battalions, Lord Kitchener raised a New Army. In this force the 6th, 7th and 8th Service Battalions of the Regiment were all engaged in the fighting in France and Flanders; like the 1st Battalion, they suffered appalling casualties in the trenches. Private Sage here won the Victoria Cross. The total casualties of the Regiment during this war were almost 10,000 men. The major Battle Honours for this war, to be carried on the Colours, were: 'Marne 1914–18', 'Aisne 1914', 'Ypres 1915, 17, 18', 'Somme 1916, 18', 'Albert 1916, 18', 'Arras 1917, 18', 'Hindenburg Line', 'Palestine 1917–18', 'Tigris 1916'.

The Second World War found the 1st Battalion in India and the 2nd in Gibraltar.[1] The 4th, 5th, 6th and 7th Battalions of the Territorial Army were mobilized in England. Both Regular battalions were for long confined to their peace-time stations; but eventually the 1st Battalion, after three months' action on the North-west Frontier, went to Burma to take part in the Arakan fighting, and the 2nd Battalion was sent to Italy; almost at once the 2nd was involved in the hard-fought crossing of the River Garigliano, suffering serious losses; later they advanced up the leg of Italy before being suddenly switched to Greece in order to prevent the Communists from gaining control.

Of all the Battalions of the Territorial Army only the 4th and 7th were selected to go into action as members of the Regiment. Both these battalions were part of the 43rd Wessex Division and took part in all the battles of the Second Front from Normandy to the River Elbe. Notable battles were fought by both battalions around Caen, on the Seine, in the Rhineland and across the Rhine. The 10th Battalion was selected for conversion to parachutists and, as the 7th Parachute (Light Infantry) Battalion, fought in Normandy and Germany. The 30th Battalion was used as garrison troops in Sicily and Italy. During the Burma campaign, Second Lieutenant C. A. Cairns won the Victoria Cross posthumously while serving away from the Regiment with the South Staffordshire Regiment. The major Battle Honours to be borne

---

[1] The five years spent by the 2nd Battalion in Gibraltar before and during the Second World War bring the total service of the Regiment in that garrison to thirty-eight years.

on the Colours for this war were: 'Hill 112', 'Mont Pincon', 'Rhineland', 'Rhine', 'North-west Europe 1944–45', 'Cassino 11', 'Cosina Canal Crossing', 'Italy 1944–45', 'North Arakan', 'Ngakyedauk Pass'.

So the Second World War came to an end and soon afterwards the 4th and 7th Battalions were simultaneously put into 'suspended animation', as the official jargon ran. The 7th Parachute (Light Infantry) Battalion lasted a little longer, but it too was eventually disbanded. This left the 1st Battalion in India and the 2nd Battalion in Greece. As the army adjusted itself to the new map that history had decided upon, this deployment of Regular battalions soon became out of date. The following chapters relate the journeys, stations and fate of the Regiment as it was sent hither and thither in furtherance of British post-war political strategy.

CHAPTER TWO

THE PAINS AND PROBLEMS OF PEACE

1st Battalion in India – *Ultimus in Indis* – 2nd Battalion
in Greece and Austria – Training organizations – The Depot
reopens at Taunton – Light Infantry Brigade Training
Centre at Cove – 1st Battalion as Light Infantry Training
Centre – Victory celebrations and war memorials – Freedoms
of Taunton and Bath – Sir John Swayne Colonel of the
Regiment – Light Infantry Standardization – Regimental
Reunion – 4th Battalion re-formed – 1st Battalion at Bordon – Lieutenant-Colonel C. S. Howard in command – 1st
Battalion at Storrington and Dover – List of office-holders –
Germany: Münster and Wuppertal – Lieutenant-Colonel
J. L. Brind in command – Preparations for Malaya – Farewell
parade at Bulford – Malayan problems – Training and reorganization at Kota Tinggi – Move to Selangor – List of
office-holders.

THE reaction of the British, after suffering the pains and
tribulations of a successful war, has ever been the same: to
reduce the armed forces. If the reaction after the defeat of
the Germans and Japanese was slower to make itself felt than
in the past, it came none the less surely. At times it looked
as if the Regiment was not to survive; in fact, the struggle
for existence was to be protracted for some thirteen years—
until 12 September 1959.

This chapter deals with the slow return to peace-time
soldiering. It relates the changes in military organizations,
as they were scrapped, altered, or even renewed as emergencies came and went, as politicians breathed hot and cold,
as the Cold War waxed and waned, as the War Office strove
vainly to achieve some sort of balance in the army: in the
one scale, what was considered to be the distribution of the

available men between the various arms necessary for a major war; in the other, the distribution necessary for the existing armed peace. Assuredly the planners were faced with a stubborn enough problem; for while all Britain's enemies, except Russia, could be instantly annihilated by nuclear weapons, these lesser enemies could never, for moral reasons, be dealt with in such a manner. They had to be dealt with by normal methods, that is to say, in the long run, by Infantry; and there was little enough Infantry available. For the Treasury, swept willy-nilly into approving millions for atomic weapons, had to try to recoup its losses elsewhere, and this meant reducing the conventional arms, above all the Infantry. The outcome was painfully apparent; the few remaining Infantry battalions were soon doing work that required double their number. The speed and frequency with which battalions moved around the trouble-spots of the Empire gathered ever-increasing momentum.

The previous volume of the Regimental History left the 1st Battalion at Shargarh in the Central Provinces of India under the command of Lieutenant-Colonel C. S. Howard. While they were there, a mutiny of Indian troops occurred at Jubbalpore. Sudden orders to move were received at 4 p.m., and by 10 p.m. the Battalion had left Shargarh, never to return. On arrival at Jubbalpore it was found that the mutineers were quite out of hand and were rioting in the town. Luckily they had no firearms, and the Battalion was at once deployed to round them up and clear the streets. This was at length successfully accomplished with no more bloodshed than a few bayonet wounds. This task achieved, the Battalion remained encamped on the race-course for some time before moving to Deolali. In February 1947 Major F. M. De Butts was placed in temporary command and in April he took the Battalion to Bombay, where the British and Indian authorities were making the final arrangements for the evacuation of the country. Here, in July 1947, Lieutenant-Colonel J. R. I. Platt assumed command.

It was a period fraught with possibilities of trouble. There was the likelihood of civil unrest; the Battalion had to produce an impeccable performance on departure; and all the time there was the nagging problem of soldiers going home on demobilization, while no replacements came out. At one time it seemed as if there might well be insufficient men for the final parade. In fact there was no civil unrest in Bombay and the desperate massacres that occurred elsewhere were mercifully absent. The transfer of authority from the British to the Indians passed without incident, largely owing to the good relations between General Whistler on the one hand and Sir Maharaj Singh on the other.

On Independence Day the 1st Battalion had the sad distinction of being the only British unit on parade with the Indian Army. Marching past the Governor, Sir John Colville, and the Prime Minister of Bombay, they received a great ovation and, indeed, 'stole the show'; it was a demonstration of the excellent relations that existed between the Regiment and the Indians.

On 28 February 1948 came the final evacuation of that great continent, the ending of an Empire. Guards of Honour were provided by the Royal Indian Navy, the 3rd Indian Grenadiers, the 1st Mahratta Light Infantry, the Second Battalion the Royal Sikh Regiment and the 3rd/5th Royal Gurkha Rifles. It was an impressive moment: a sad and moving ceremony. The 1st Battalion, woefully depleted, but rising nobly to the high standard required of such an occasion, slow-marched proudly and impeccably through the Gateway of India. Motor launches awaited them: the Colours whipped out in the breeze as they were taken off to the waiting troopship. At least this Empire had passed away with dignity and decorum. This momentous occasion is commemorated by the silver replica of the Gateway of India presented to Lieutenant-Colonel Platt by representatives of the Indian Government.

The 1st Battalion arrived in England on 17 March 1948. A message of welcome was received from King George VI, the Colonel-in-Chief, and the Battalion was personally welcomed by the Adjutant-General and the Lord Mayor of Liverpool. Going straight to Taunton, they paraded through the town with Colours flying, the first battalion of the Regiment to avail themselves of the newly-granted Freedom of the Borough. They had been overseas for twenty-one years, nineteen of them in India. It is noteworthy that one member of the Regiment, Sergeant Cotton, had served with them continuously for twenty years without once returning home.

The 2nd Battalion was in Greece under the command of Lieutenant-Colonel A. Hunt throughout 1946, based initially on Komotini in Thrace, the most easterly province, and later on Serres in Western Macedonia. Southern Greece had been largely pacified and most of the Communist insurgents had now been driven northwards into the mountainous area along the frontier with Turkey and Bulgaria. The country was still very unsettled and the Greek police and army were in the process of reforming after their war-time misfortunes. The Battalion's role was to maintain peace in these remote provinces and to assist the Greek forces in preventing murderous forays by the rebels. In order to provide a visible sign of their presence and to give encouragement to the villagers, the Battalion carried out company 'Flag Marches' into the remote countryside, taking with them Red Cross parcels for the poverty-stricken natives; unfortunately many of these parcels had originally been intended for the Indian Army and some items, such as curry powder, were not appreciated. Although the rebels created many incidents, the Battalion was never directly involved in any of them. When the first Greek national elections were held, the officers of the Battalion were employed as neutral observers at the polling booths. This happened again later, during the plebiscite which resulted in the return of King George of Greece.

Lieutenant-Colonel J. F. Snow assumed command at the end of 1946 and in February 1947 the Battalion embarked at Salonika for Austria. Arriving at Trieste, the Battalion was welcomed by General Sir John Harding, the Commander-in-Chief of this troubled international zone, and then went on by train to Volkermacht in the Austrian province of Carinthia. Once again they were keeping the peace in a disturbed land. Companies were spread along the Yugoslav frontier as far as Wolfsberg, where it adjoined Hungary. It was a mountainous area among the Karawanken Mountains, through which ran the River Drava. The duties of the Battalion included patrolling to prevent illegal crossing of the frontier, the reception of train loads of Displaced Persons and their despatch to camps in the interior, the running of a Prisoner-of-War camp and even the provision of men for the distasteful task of firing squads. Relations with Yugoslavia were strained and there was little friendliness along the frontier. One patrol, straying accidentally into Yugoslavia, was detained for some time before being released.

The Battalion took its turn in providing the ceremonial guards and duties in Vienna; this was a testing tour in a capital city and as the cynosure of the four Allied Military Governments. The highlight of this tour for the Battalion was mounting guard and sounding Retreat at Schönbrunn Palace before the Allied generals and their staffs.

On 21 February the Battalion left Austria for England, arriving in the middle of the night after a dreary journey at Didcot. In April they moved to Bordon where, by 23 June 1948, the first stage in the reduction of the Infantry by the formal amalgamation of the 1st and 2nd Battalions into the 1st Battalion had taken place. The commander of this Battalion was Lieutenant-Colonel J. F. Snow. But in fact, as will be seen, it was not a real battalion.

The various war-time training establishments took some time to disappear. But eventually the 16th Infantry Training Centre at Colchester, and the 16th Infantry Holding Battalion at Plymouth, were closed, and in their stead was formed the 13th Primary Training Centre at Taunton to which in due course was added a small Depot staff. This reinforced Major F. M. Turner, who had been the sole guardian of Regimental interests throughout the war and had protected the Depot against all comers, including a wave of civilian 'squatters'. Although this new training centre was at Taunton, it did not necessarily train men for the Regiment.

In April 1948 the Light Infantry Training Centre was formed at Cove, near Aldershot, and was responsible for training men for all the Light Infantry Regiments. This was a vast improvement but, even after the introduction of the new system, it is recorded that drafts en route for Light Infantry battalions were stolen before they could arrive. Assuredly it was essential that the training units should be linked with the active battalions they served, for all too often during the late war men of the Regiment, arriving in a theatre of operations in which a battalion was serving, were drafted to some other regiment, while the battalion on the very same day received men from a different regiment. At one time during the war there was a Somerset Irish in Italy and a Somerset Scottish in Normandy. Now, slowly, this sort of thing was being stopped, to the benefit of all. Obviously the forming of the Light Infantry Brigade, and similar brigades of other regiments, enormously assisted the problem of drafting by broadening the basis of the groups to which men belonged. It not only broadened the area from which they came but also the number of units to which they could be sent and yet remain in the family.

The forming of the Light Infantry Training Centre at Cove did away with the Primary Training Centre at Taunton, so that once again the Depot dwindled to almost nothing, and Lieutenant-Colonel Hunt with a minute nucleus was hard put to it to try to make the Depot the home and heart of the Regiment. It was not, in fact, until 1951 that the Depot was opened again in order to train men for the Regiment and for the rest of the Light Infantry Brigade.

The Light Infantry Brigade Training Centre moved to Bordon in April 1948, and in June the 1st Battalion arrived to take over the duties of the training centre. The Battalion had to try to retain its identity, while at the same time serving the whole Light Infantry Brigade with equal loyalty and training recruits for all—no easy task. It was happily made easier by the close bond of comradeship that already existed between the various Light Infantry Regiments, which had been fostered by the Colonels of the Regiments between the wars, long before the army had thought of grouping regiments regionally or according to their traditions. In this the Light Infantry had a long lead over the rest of the Infantry and the compulsory fusion caused remarkably little friction.

While the Regiment was suffering the pangs of reorganization as a result of peace, a series of ceremonies were held to commemorate and celebrate war and victory. In June 1946 the Victory Parade was held in London, in which were carried the 4th Battalion Colours, escorted by representative detachments from those battalions still in being who were within reach. On 27 August 1946 General G. I. Thomas, the wartime commander of the 43rd Division, unveiled a memorial to the men of this division on Hill 112 in Normandy. This was the site of the first major battle of this division, in which both the 4th and the 7th Battalions had served; the 4th Battalion had suffered particularly severe casualties in this battle.

On 8 June 1946 the Regiment was presented with the Freedom of the Borough of Taunton. Detachments were made available by devious means, in order that as many battalions as possible should be represented. After the official ceremony in Vivary Park, the Regiment marched through the streets of the town and was then entertained at luncheon by the mayor and councillors. At the same time, the newly installed carillon in the parish church of Saint Mary Magdalene was dedicated, being set in motion by Major Whitehead with the tune of Bunyan's hymn 'To be a Pilgrim', as a special memorial to the men of the 7th Battalion; this tune had been adopted during the Battle of Britain by Lieutenant-Colonel A. E. Snow as the 7th Battalion hymn and has since often been considered the Regimental hymn.

On 3 April 1948 the Regiment was honoured with the Freedom of the City of Bath. Detachments of the 1st, 2nd and 4th Battalions and the Depot were on parade under Colonel

J. F. Snow. A large gathering of members of the Regiment and their friends were present. The day ended with festive dancing in the Guildhall.

Decisions on the form of the Regimental War Memorial were put into effect in 1949 when, at the Annual Remembrance Day Parade at Taunton, the Book of Remembrance was dedicated at Saint Mary Magdalene's Church. The decision to provide two rooms at the Union Jack Club in London held fire, although the funds were available, owing to post-war building restrictions, and not until December 1952 were the two rooms ready.

On 15 October 1947 Major-General V. H. B. Majendie relinquished the Colonelcy of the Regiment after a tenure of nine years and was replaced by Lieutenant-General Sir John Swayne. But for the mischance of ill health, General Swayne would have been Adjutant-General to the Forces while acting as Colonel of the Regiment, like his pre-war predecessor, Sir Walter Braithwaite.

On 22 January 1947 a most important step towards the preservation and consolidation of Light Infantry traditions was taken by the Colonel's Committee. This was the standardization of Light Infantry drill throughout the Brigade. Previously each regiment had interpreted Light Infantry movements in their own way. Not only did this standardization facilitate the training of recruits in the various regimental depots and ensure the easy interchange of officers and men within the Brigade, but—more important—this decision, affecting the outward manifestation of Light Infantry, welded the regiments into an ever more firmly knit fraternity. Later a similar agreement was reached on the standardization of dress within the Brigade.

On 16 April 1949 the first Regimental Reunion since before the war was held at the Depot at Taunton. Many hundreds of members from all branches of the Association, travelling from all over Britain, assembled on the barrack square. The doyen of this great assembly was ex-Colour Sergeant Bull who, ninety-three years old, paraded wearing his Zulu War medals.

H.M. King George VI, Colonel-in-Chief of the Regiment

Ultimus in Indis: The 1st Battalion passing through the Gateway of In
Bombay

The 1st Battalion Colours embark for England

This gathering was a particular success owing to the reconstitution of the Association which, originating as the Old Comrades in 1910 had been revitalized by a new charter in 1946. A reunion has taken place biennially ever since under the stage management of Mr Holt, the general secretary of the Association.

The 4th Battalion, which had been put into 'suspended animation' in October 1946, was re-formed on 1 April 1947. The headquarters were at Bath with companies at Yeovil, Taunton and Wellington, Midsomer Norton, Glastonbury and Wells. Lieutenant-Colonel W. Q. Roberts was its first post-war commander. In March 1948 the Battalion had made such good progress that they were able to provide a Guard of Honour for Her Royal Highness Princess Margaret at Bath, and on 31 October 1948 they sent a detachment to London for a review of the Territorial Army by His Majesty King George VI. On 21 May 1949 they provided a Guard of Honour at the unveiling of a War Memorial to the 43rd Division by General Sir Ivor Thomas on the top of Castle Hill at Mere, overlooking three Wessex counties: Somerset, Wiltshire and Dorset. For the unveiling on 20 September 1952 of the final memorial to the 43rd Division, erected at Wynard's Gap near Crewkerne, Bandmaster Golledge and Bugle-Major Wiltshire took the 4th Battalion Band and Bugles to perform at the ceremony.

The 1st Battalion spent the year 1949 at Bordon, training drafts for the other Light Infantry battalions. In accordance with the new policy of strengthening the Brigade spirit the Battalion was by no means entirely Somerset Light Infantry. Officers, Warrant officers and Non-Commissioned officers from all the other regiments were on the strength of the Battalion, and similarly the Regiment had many serving with the other regiments of the Brigade.

On May 1 1949 they provided a Guard of Honour for the Queen of Siam, returning to her country with the ashes of her husband, the late King of Siam. On 24 August 1949 they were visited by the Secretary of State for War in the Labour

Government, Emmanuel Shinwell, and on 11 October by the
Prime Minister, Clement Attlee—one of the very few occa-
sions on which the Regiment has been visited by a Prime
Minister.

In June 1949 Lieutenant-Colonel J. F. Snow handed over
command of the 1st Battalion to Lieutenant-Colonel C. S.
Howard, who thus became for the second time commanding
officer of this battalion. His total tenure of command, some
six years, cannot however compare with that of commanders
of an earlier age: Ogilvie's of sixteen years from 1765 to
1781: Sale's of thirteen years from 1830 to 1843: Lord Mark
Kerr's of eleven years from 1854 to 1865. Nevertheless,
Colonel Howard achieved a rare distinction.

In June 1950 the 1st Battalion was relieved of its duties
as Light Infantry training battalion by the 1st Battalion the
Duke of Cornwall's Light Infantry and became an active
battalion again at Storrington in Sussex. At once they were
dispersed: some to guard United States airfields, some to
provide assistance at the annual Territorial Army camps in
the south-east. Eventually they all concentrated at Old Park
Barracks, Dover. Here, in November 1950, they provided a
Guard of Honour on the occasion of the State visit by Her
Majesty Queen Juliana of the Netherlands. This somewhat
negative soldiering came to an end in January 1951, when
they went to join the British Army of the Rhine at Münster
in Germany. This was to be real soldiering again with a full-
strength battalion training for a possible European war.

The following were the principal office-holders at this time:

Commanding Officer .	Lieutenant-Colonel C.S. Howard, O.B.E.
Adjutant . . .	Captain P. J. Bush
Quartermaster . .	Major R. H. P. Fortnum, M.B.E.
R.S.M. . . .	R.S.M. K. E. Bartlett
Headquarter Company	Major E. H. I. Webber
	C.S.M. C. E. Samson

A Company	. .	Major G. W. Stead
		C.S.M. E. A. Giles, M.M.
B Company	. .	Major J. C. Liesching (D.C.L.I.)
		C.S.M. E. T. Mullen
C Company	. .	Captain P. H. E. Borwick
		C.S.M. A. Morris
D Company	. .	Major H. McLean
		C.S.M. W. J. Shelton
Support Company	.	Major R. A. St G. Martin, M.B.E.
		(43rd, 52nd L.I.)
		C.S.M. J. Doherty
Bandmaster	. .	Bandmaster W. H. Moore,
		A.R.C.M.

The British Army of the Rhine had long ceased to be an occupying force and was now the nation's defensive shield already deployed in Europe against possible Russian aggression. It did not stand alone, but was closely integrated with the armies of England's allies engaged in the same defensive role. In this army, as in previous British Expeditionary Forces, was the preponderance of the active units: they were equipped and trained on the most up-to-date lines. In the Cold War their very presence and state of training had its politico-strategical value and in the event of war they would expect to be instantly engaged. This was the army, then, that the 1st Battalion joined. Despite diversions to help the Territorials and guard American bomber bases, Lieutenant-Colonel Howard had not allowed the previous six months to be wasted. Every available moment had been used to bring a training battalion up to a state of efficiency that would enable it to take its place in this front-line army without undue strain. While at Storrington emphasis had been on individual training, particularly of specialists; at Dover emphasis had been on company training, which had culminated in a ten days' intensive period of manoeuvres at the Practical Training Area at Stanford in Suffolk. This paid a handsome dividend on arrival in Germany.

Arriving in Germany in January 1951 they were accommodated at Oxford Barracks, Münster. These ex-Luftwaffe barracks were admirably comfortable and convenient, quite unlike any barracks in England; and in addition there were a host of Germans, both men and women, to do the chores, thus enabling almost every man to concentrate on training. The married men were also very well cared for, with admirable quarters and adequate domestic help. The actual cost of living was low, but the standard was high, so that human nature being what it is, the general opinion was that living was dear.

The arrival of the Battalion so early in the year was fortunate, for it meant that they had until May to prepare for the rigours of the subsequent training season. In May company and battalion manœuvres started, August and September were devoted to brigade and divisional manœuvres, October to army manœuvres. Training was almost constant, and a married man was lucky if he had more than one long week-end a month in his comfortable home. By and large the unmarried men thoroughly enjoyed the manœuvres, living in the open, in bivouacs or tents; the married men could hardly be expected to be so enthusiastic. Training was carried out initially at Borkenberge, where the Battalion ran an almost permanent company group camp on the edge of an attractive lake. This area was not only used for training but also as a Battalion holiday camp where the men could relax on the lakeside. More advanced company group training was carried out at Haltern, but really serious training took place at Sennelager, in Lippe, at the All-Arms Training Centre. There advanced exercises with tanks, the Royal Air Force and artillery, all firing live ammunition, could be carried out up to battalion level. Very soon all ranks had got to know each of the three areas only too intimately.

Many of the exercises were most exciting and were thoroughly enjoyed by everyone. Emphasis was at that time on the company group system, and detachments of Support Company were attached for long periods to rifle companies, which added interest to the tactical manœuvring. One notable exercise was against the Norwegian and Danish contingents in the Allied army; another involving Welsh Guards and the Royal Tank Regiment was both exciting and profitable. The culmination of the training cycle for 1951 was the great Exercise 'Counter-Thrust', in which about 100,000 men from all the Allied armies took part. This entailed moving many hundreds of miles, partly by lorry, but much of it on foot, up the length of Germany. The Battalion was chiefly engaged in the Fallingbostel and Soltau area, where they earned considerable kudos by outwitting the umpires. An interesting feature of these manœuvres was the complete lack of restrictions on the use of land: claims officers followed in rear of the advance and settled the claim then and there. Providing that the soldiers showed reasonable restraint and common sense, there was little or no hostility on the part of the German farmers.

Early in 1952 there was a re-deployment of the 6th Infantry Brigade, including the 1st Battalion, who were moved south to Wuppertal in the Ruhr so as to be closer to the rest of the 2nd Infantry Division. This meant exchanging rural surroundings for an industrial area; but training went on unabated. Indeed, training was everything and even sport took a very secondary place. One interesting sport was beagling—not yet outlawed by the Germans, who have their own method of hunting the hare—and the Battalion ran a pack of hounds inherited from the Durham Light Infantry. General Sir John Harding became Commander-in-Chief of the Rhine Army while the Battalion was in Germany. The Battalion provided a Guard of Honour at Bad Oeynhausen on his arrival. He visited the Battalion several times, choosing to use a helicopter for these visits and thus introduced a new element into military life which has since become almost commonplace.

On 7 April 1952 Lieutenant-Colonel C. S. Howard handed over command of the 1st Battalion to Lieutenant-Colonel J. L. Brind. Training continued at the same high pressure but with a bias towards the Malayan jungles, where the Battalion now knew it would be going at the end of the year. The fir forests of Germany were transformed by an effort of imagination into the jungles of Malaya and, if this proved in fact too much for the average imagination, at least every man now had his eyes turned towards a definite future and would arrive in the East with his mind attuned to the change. Meanwhile, intensive reorganization was required so that those men ineligible for Malaya, owing to inadequate remaining length of service, could be sent elsewhere and replacements posted in their stead. In this way some 269 men were posted away and some 236 new men were received. The Battalion was now 66 per cent composed of National Servicemen. At the same time Colonel Brind strengthened his officer cadre by arranging for many senior officers, who had been away from the Regiment over long, to return at once and for others to follow.

On 4 September 1952 the Battalion returned to England for embarkation leave and refitting at Carter Barracks, Bulford. On 17 September a large advance-party sailed for Malaya including all the company commanders, who were to attend a jungle training course before the Battalion arrived. On 16 October 1952 the outgoing Chief of the Imperial General Staff, Sir William Slim, visited the Battalion during a final rehearsal for the farewell parade during which he addressed the men. On 25 October the parade took place before a great concourse of friends, Territorials and members of the Regimental Association. General Sir John Harding, who had already been appointed the next Chief of the Imperial General Staff, inspected the parade which he addressed. On 27 October 1952 the Battalion sailed from Southampton under the Second-in-command, Major De Butts. Lieutenant-Colonel Brind and the Quartermaster, Major Smart, remained behind to fly out later and to arrive before the Battalion.

On 24 November the Battalion disembarked at Singapore and moved at once to a training camp on the mainland at

Kota Tinggi. This was the home of the Malayan Jungle Fighting Training Centre, where each battalion on arrival spent two months. During this period they went out on training patrols in the adjacent jungle, drew their special equipment, vehicles and weapons, and became somewhat acclimatized to the damp and heat.

There was an immense amount to do and to learn. The weapons with which the men were equipped were quite different from those in use in Europe and as the vital jungle slogan was 'Shoot to kill', practice with them was all-important. The vehicles too were different, as were the wireless sets. More signallers were required than in Europe, and they had to be trained in the use of morse, as reception by voice was often impossible. Men had to be selected and trained as dog-handlers. Support Company, except for the Mortar Platoon, had virtually no specialist role and these men had to be turned into riflemen; later this company was to be transformed into a training organization for drafts of new men coming out from England. Each rifleman also had much to learn: how to live in the jungle and remain efficient; how to lay an ambush; how to react if ambushed; jungle navigation by map and compass and, of course, 'Shoot to kill'. There was also a strange new language in use by the Security Forces which had to be learnt. To a newcomer it was an incomprehensible jargon mostly composed of meaningless abbreviations. Even a place-name such as Kuala Lumpur, the capital, was shortened to K.L. As for the abbreviations of police and other official titles, the uninitiated needed a glossary; he could hardly guess that the 'Officer Supervising Police Circle' or the 'Chief Special Branch Officer', complicated enough titles anyway, were respectively known as O.S.P.C. and C.S.B.O.

The tented camp at Kota Tinggi was poor; no lighting, no proper drainage and no proper roads. It was the monsoon season and nothing could be kept dry. So bad were the conditions that representations made by Colonel Brind resulted in the whole system of training and equipping newly arrived battalions being changed. But Major Smart, the Quarter-master, and his assistants, competing with these adverse conditions, somehow managed to administer the Battalion, draw all the new equipment, and arrange Christmas celebrations.

Colonel Brind had decided not to take the families out with the Battalion. They were to join later, when the Battalion had found its feet. This meant that married men would be able to concentrate solely on their new tasks without being worried by family problems. This was probably a wise decision from the operational as well as from the family point of view.

Tactical advance parties left for their operational bases on 1 January 1953, and the whole Battalion moved from Johore to Selangor on 7 January to take up their new duties.

The following were the principal office-holders in the 1st Battalion on arrival in Malaya:

Commanding Officer .	Lieutenant-Colonel J. L. Brind, D.S.O.
Second-in-command .	Major F. M. De Butts, M.B.E.
Adjutant . . .	Captain A. J. Collyns
Quartermaster . .	Major C. W. Smart, M.B.E.
R.S.M. . . .	R.S.M. K. E. Bartlett
Headquarter Company	Major D. J. R. Parker
	C.S.M. F. J. Bowden
	C.S.M. R. Harton (K.S.L.I.)
A Company . .	Major G. W. Stead
	C.S.M. E. A. Giles, M.M.
B Company . .	Major J. L. Waddy
	C.S.M. E. W. Broadbent
C Company . .	Major P. H. E. Borwick
	C.S.M. A. J. Longney
D Company . .	Major J. J. Ogilvie
	C.S.M. H. W. J. Joiner (K.S.L.I.)
Support Company .	Captain E. J. Kingston
	C.S.M. F. C. Perkins
Bandmaster . .	Bandmaster W. H. Moore, A.R.C.M.

Scale of Miles

0   20   40   60   80   100

MAP 1
MALAYA

SIAM

KEDAH

Kota Bahru

SOUTH

CHINA

SEA

George Town
PROVINCE
WELLESLEY
PENANG

PERAK

KELANTAN

TRENGGANU

Ipoh

PAHANG

Benta   Kuala
         Lipis

Raub

Kuantan

Kuala Kubu Bahru   Mentekab

Bentong   Temerloh   Pahang River

Triang

Kuala Lumpur

Kuala
Selangor

SELANGOR

Klang

Telok   Kajang
Datok

Sepang

Port Dixon

NEGRI

Seremban

SEMBILAN

STRAITS

MALACCA

JOHORE

N

OF

Malacca

Kota
Tinggi

MALACCA

Johore Bahru

SINGAPORE

REFERENCE

International Boundary   — · — · —

State Boundary   — · · — · · —

CHAPTER THREE

MALAYA: THE NORTH SWAMP[1]

Operational picture – War by committee – Communist organizations – First successes – An important success – The jungle – The jungle swamp – Life in base and on patrol.

THE war, or the emergency, as it was officially called, was going well. The Security Forces were definitely getting the upper hand. No longer were untrained and inexperienced troops blundering about the jungles fighting periodic stand-up battles with formed bodies of terrorists. There was now a wealth of jungle-lore and knowledge of Communist tactics on which to draw. The soldiers were dressed, armed and equipped for their specific tasks. The Royal Air Force was now able and prepared to help. The police were in adequate strength and mostly reliable. The Special Branch officers were men of vast experience at their secret game and had built up an ever-growing system of informers. Co-operation between the civil authorities and the armed forces was excellent. The native Chinese population could at last be persuaded, in certain circumstances, to help. The bandits, although prepared for and capable of fighting if cornered, were mostly lying low. Although the Battalion could not expect to kill as many terrorists as had battalions operating in the days of bandit plenitude, it had arrived at a propitious moment.

The Malayan Emergency was a perfect example of 'war by committee'. At each level of the civilian, police and military hierarchy was a joint committee, which meeting daily at what was generally known as 'Morning Prayers', discussed and made decisions on all aspects of the operations then in progress. At this meeting decisions might variously be made on a bombing strike, patrolling in a certain area, a police cordon,

[1] See Maps One and Two.

food control regulations, or the clearing of an overgrown rubber estate. Those present were invariably the head civilian administrator, the chief policeman, the senior soldier, and the head of the local Special Branch. Other people, such as members of the information services or planters, might be co-opted from time to time. Sometimes the planters would all be invited to a special meeting where they would be told about the operations in progress so that they might both co-operate and be encouraged.

This committee system was the basis on which the whole campaign was run and, however much the soldier might be irked by civilian restrictions, he could only overcome them by persuasion; for the army was there only 'in support of the civil power'. The soldiers who attended these meetings had a heavy responsibility to ensure that their particular committee did work, did co-operate, was helpful; and this could only be achieved by tact, patience and firmness. This was, of course, quite right, for the army was not operating alone, nor could it achieve success on its own. Without the information provided by Special Branch, patrols would have blundered about utterly in the dark. Without firm food control by police units, the bandits would have had no supply difficulties. Without the rules and regulations promulgated by the District Officer, there would have been no legal control whatsoever.

Without a doubt the Malayan Races Liberation Army (M.R.L.A.)—the high-sounding title of the bandits—made a grave blunder when after the war they decided to take to the jungle. To have bided their time, while infiltrating into schools and trade unions, would have made them much more dangerous, insidious and difficult to combat. As it was, they had built up a terrorist organization that suited their purposes most adequately. At the bottom of the organization were the 'Masses' Executives', sympathizers and supporters in the villages. Their job was to provide food, medicine, clothes and so on, when told to do so. Above them were the 'Min Yuen' who collected these supplies and either used

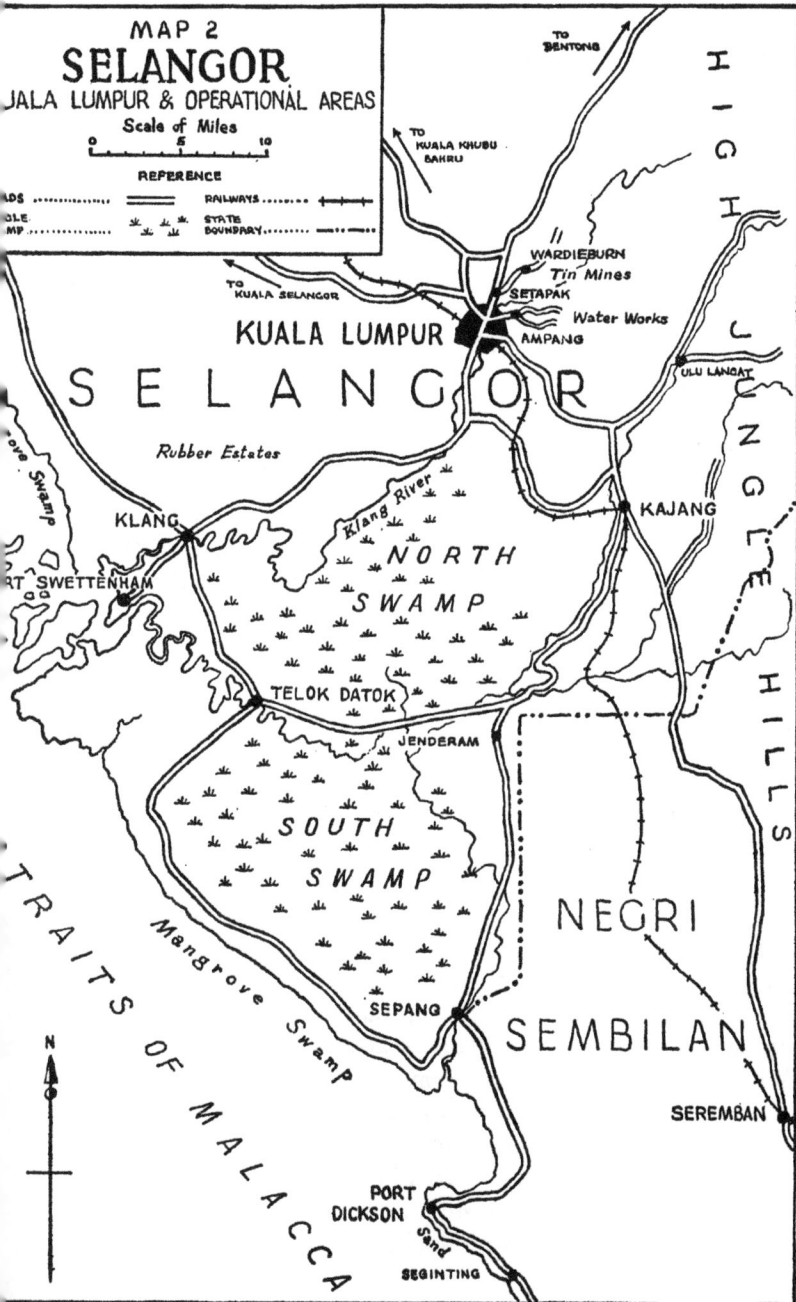

MAP 2
SELANGOR
JALA LUMPUR & OPERATIONAL AREAS
Scale of Miles
0   5   10

REFERENCE
ADS ....   RAILWAYS .... +—+—+
OLE ....   STATE
MP ....   BOUNDARY .... —·—·—·—

TO BENTONG

TO KUALA KHUBU BAHRU

WARDIEBURN
Tin Mines

SETAPAK

Water Works

TO KUALA SELANGOR

KUALA LUMPUR

AMPANG

ULU LANGAT

SELANGOR

Rubber Estates

ove Swamp

KLANG

Klang River

KAJANG

T SWETTENHAM

N O R T H

S W A M P

TELOK DATOK

JENDERAM

S O U T H

S W A M P

NEGRI

SEPANG

SEMBILAN

Mangrove Swamp

H I G H   J U N G L E   H I L L S

SEREMBAN

S T R A I T S   O F   M A L A C C A

PORT DICKSON

Sand

SEGINTING

N

them themselves or passed them on to their superiors. These 'Min Yuen' did not normally live deep in the jungle, but camped on the jungle fringes near their supply villages. Over these groups were the brains of the organization divided into Branches, Districts, States and National groups according to their importance. These were run by secretaries, hard-bitten, hard-core Communists, who lived deep in the jungle with a small bodyguard and a few specialists. The area system was very rigid and no bandit force might move out of its area without permission from above, which was normally refused. In addition to these area organizations, there were normally independent platoons of killers. They were well armed and trained, and were responsible for serious atrocities such as ambushes and murders. They lived deep in the jungle.

The weakness of this system was that it was most vulnerable where it could be struck at in the open, that is, at the sympathizers in the villages. If Special Branch could eliminate the 'Masses' Executives', the 'Min Yuen' would be forced to take risks to obtain supplies which would give the soldiers, the police and even the Home Guard an opportunity for ambushes. The more the 'Min Yuen' and their suppliers could be hampered, the shorter would become the whole organization of supplies, and then the senior bandits would be forced into taking risks. This would produce more opportunities for attack. Moreover, with their rigid territorial boundaries, they could not go elsewhere, so that starvation, acts of desperation or surrender would in theory be their eventual lot. But to bring about this theoretical situation there would be months of Special Branch preparatory work, months of apparently fruitless patrolling, many bitter disappointments. There would come times when all would be convinced that there were no bandits at all in the area; times when all were convinced that Special Branch were pursuing a chimera. These were times to keep a cool head and an equable temper for a sudden lucky break might produce a kill; a surrender might follow; perhaps another kill as a result of information from the ex-bandit. By then the terrorists would be worried, always on the move lest their camps, hide-outs and routes were about to be betrayed and, if all went well, the climax would be pretty swift, ending with the complete elimination of a bandit organization in a certain area. In this connection the elimination of terrorist couriers was an important factor. A vital element in the terrorist organization was a sound courier system with absolutely safe rendezvous. This they ensured by restricting to a minimum the knowledge of bandits selected for each task. This was effective enough if a courier surrendered or was captured, or if instructions were found in a letter box, for all that the Security Forces got was a direction such as 'Meet at the place where Ah Pee cooked the iguana' with a series of dates spread over several weeks: information of maddening insufficiency. But if it baffled the Security Forces, it also meant that, if the courier failed for any reason to keep his rendezvous, it set off a chain of reactions amongst the terrorists themselves. Being uncertain of the reason for his failure to turn up at the appointed place, they had to fear the worst and assume that he had defected and would be used against them. It also meant that their own communication security system had cut them off from one another, and it might take months to effect a meeting; in some cases they never succeeded in regaining contact. It is easy then to imagine the state of nervous expectancy to which they could be reduced, if things were going badly. This probably accounts for the snowball effect once a terrorist band was on the run.

The first operation in which the Battalion was engaged followed this pattern. The 1st Battalion the Suffolk Regiment, from whom the 1st Battalion took over, had had an exceptionally fine record during their tour in Malaya and their final operation had been prepared and conducted with great skill. The Battalion took over this successful operation and almost at once had a run of astonishing successes. This operation concerned an area of jungle swamp south-west of the capital, Kuala Lumpur, of some 1,000 square miles. The

31

main target in the area was Number One Platoon M.R.L.A. This platoon, commanded by Liew Siew Fook, was about twenty-five strong and operated in the Telok Datok area known as the North Swamp. It was supported by 'Min Yuen' groups based on the village of Jendaram. As the operation had already been in progress for some time, this platoon was now hard pressed. Lieutenant-Colonel Brind at once concentrated both B and C Companies and a company of the Worcestershire Regiment, and in due course arranged for the police to screen the offending village and remove the food-supplying sympathizers.

Events were not slow to warm up. To begin with, two members of Number One Platoon surrendered, one of them bringing with him the only light machine-gun remaining to the platoon. This was a good start. On 26 January Lieutenant R. E. Waight was able to carry out a successful ambush that resulted in the wounding and capture of a District Committee member and the capture of three others. One, a woman, escaped later under pretext of urinating; the soldiers were still too honest, or simple, to credit such behaviour. Luckily she gave herself up later. Next day Lieutenant H. Atkinson attacked a camp after crawling for the last hour through a swamp; he killed one terrorist and captured another. On the following day a patrol under Sergeant Beaumont killed two more; unfortunately Beaumont was himself killed at the first exchange of fire. This was a sad loss of a trained patrol leader with previous experience of fighting in Malaya. Luckily Lance-Corporal Griffiths took charge at once and led a chase in which the bandits were slain. Atkinson was not to be stopped; on 7 February he contacted four bandits, killed one and wounded another. Unfortunately another sad loss occurred here in the death of Private Alan Johnson, the leading scout, at the early age of 19.

During this period the harassing of areas in which troops were not operating was carried out by the Royal Navy, which shelled the jungle from off-shore, and by artillery shoots. Although this type of support was obviously wasteful, it pre-

The 2nd Battalion Bugles, Schönbrunn Palace, Vienna

H.R.H. Princess Margaret visits the 4th Battalion, Bath

Malaya: A helicopter landing zone

Disembarking from a helicopter

vented bandits from slipping off into deep jungle with impunity and restricted the areas in which they might be found. There is no doubt that it helped to make the terrorists more accessible targets to the patrols in the swamp.

Congratulations were showered upon a Battalion which was doing so spectacularly well in its first engagements. General Templer, the High Commissioner, and Major-General Stockwell, the ground force commander, both sent messages of appreciation.

The fruit of these successes was not slow to ripen, for Liew Siew Fook himself with two followers surrendered. This was not only an important fact in itself, but was of great interest to the Battalion. They were now to see how a high-ranking, hard-core bandit reacted when he surrendered. He looked, as indeed he was, a killer: crafty, clever, tough, wiry, and utterly unabashed. This leading Communist proved quite prepared to lead his late enemies back into the jungle to help to kill the chief Communist in the whole of South Selangor, Lau Cheng, a member of the State Committee. This attitude, frequently to be met with later in other terrorist leaders, is barely comprehensible to the Christian mind of the average Westerner and, although the Security Forces gratefully availed themselves of these opportunities, it can hardly be said that it endeared the bandits to the soldier. Not only was Liew Siew Fook prepared to lead the Battalion back to kill Lau Cheng but, more remarkable, the killing was achieved. On 2 March the platoons of Lieutenant D. R. Goddard, Lieutenant R. E. Waight and Lieutenant H. Atkinson successfully manœuvred to bring about Lau Cheng's death. In this engagement Lau Cheng and one bodyguard were killed and six other members of his party in the camp surrendered. Only one got away and he surrendered twenty days later. This was a startlingly successful coup.

This operation, lasting in all only five months, completely cleared the North Swamp of terrorists by eliminating the fighting Number One Platoon M.R.L.A., the South Selangor State Committee and all their supporting 'Min Yuen' groups.

It was a splendid start to the Battalion's tour in Malaya. Following what was in the opinion of some the deplorable competitive system in force in Malaya, this score of nine terrorists went to C Company, commanded by Major P. H. E. Borwick. The idea of regarding the killing of bandits as a competitive sport was to many incompatible with professional soldiering. In any case the score bore little relation to the work put in to produce the kill, as so many other factors and forces were at work. After this, C Company went four whole months without seeing a bandit; this was but typical of these operations and serves to illustrate how difficult it was for the man on patrol to be unceasingly alert for the fleeting moment.

While C Company was gaining fame, the other companies were not without their successes. A Company, at Sepang, was responsible for the South Swamp. Here Lieutenant R. A. Douglas took part in two incidents that earned him the Military Cross. On the first occasion, while lying in wait for a bandit food-collecting party outside a village, he was most unlucky in failing to kill them. On the second, he personally stalked and killed a terrorist who was hailing his comrades— he was presumably lost—after a long and skilful approach through the swamp. Lieutenant D. R. McMurtrie of B Company ambushed and killed two terrorists in a rubber plantation. Lieutenant O. J. M. Eley, commanding a D Company platoon, laid an ambush of a bandit supply point with some Chinese lumberjacks and killed one man.

The number of kills was steadily rising; but so were the number of patrol hours which appeared to have achieved nothing. The Battalion was operating in two very different types of terrain. D Company were engaged in an area that might be called classical jungle. This was a hilly area with patrols always struggling up or slithering down steep jungle-clad ridges. In the valleys were swift and almost pleasant streams. This was primary jungle, untouched by man and normally pretty easy to move through. It was often cold at night on the top of the ridges. Below this primary jungle

34

was secondary growth, where the original giant trees had been felled and a well-nigh impenetrable thicket of scrub, creepers and fern had grown up; this was often the area chosen by the 'Min Yuen' for their camps. Into both these areas ran logging trails and at their head worked Chinese loggers who, unless prevented, were food suppliers to the bandits; their presence was a constant annoyance to patrol leaders. Outside the jungle were rubber estates where from dawn until about noon Chinese and Tamil tappers were engaged in collecting the rubber latex; these again were often compelled to supply the bandits and many of them could be relied upon to give warning of the approach of soldiers by singing or clashing their collecting pots. Patrols normally had to be clear of the rubber before the tappers arrived which meant, in fact, before dawn.

The other companies were in the jungle swamps. Here sluggish, brown and crocodile-infested rivers flowed through the foul morass, where a man might wade all day in the thick liquid up to his knees, thighs or even waist. In this humid atmosphere progress was desperately slow and exhausting and was measured in hundreds of yards an hour, and not very many hundreds at that. The terrorists built themselves camps on log platforms resting on the boles of the gigantic trees. They would have a cook-house and living huts covered with a type of palm frond called Attap, and a couple of sentry posts. There would probably be a log path leading in and out of the camp. To find a camp was hard enough, for tracks were soon swallowed up by the swamp; but, once found, it was even harder to attack. One of the rules for attacking a camp was 'wait for a rainstorm'; but first find the camp. If the patrol were to try to surround the camp, they would inevitably be heard sloshing through the swamp. If they made a frontal attack, the bandits would bolt by the back door. The successes already related must be pictured in these conditions.

The jungle has been variously called a 'green Hell' or even 'neutral'. It was certainly no Hell; it was decidedly not neutral. Ferocious tigers and rampaging elephants were most unlikely to attack a patrol, although recruits had generally to be weaned of this fear. Snakes were often seen, but they never attacked. Monkeys barking and crying in the tree-tops or squabbling with the giant hornbills for nuts could sound to the newcomer like a ravening bear or tiger. No, most of the trouble came from insects. Mosquitoes and ants made ambushes a purgatory; leeches had to be burnt off at each halt. But worst of all were the hornets, wasps and bees, the angriest and fiercest in the world, and few patrols escaped without someone being badly stung about the eyes, face or neck. The cry 'Hornets!' broke the best disciplined patrol.

A description of a typical company base and of the life of a patrol may be of interest. The camp itself was generally tented, with a few simple wooden and tin erections for cookhouses and mess rooms, set in a clearing near the jungle or in a rubber plantation. It was reasonably airy and light. It could never be described as comfortable. The off-duty patrols would be in the base camp replacing torn jungle clothes, playing football, basket-ball and badminton. They would eat and sleep their fill and lounge about in the sunshine; for a week in the jungle makes an Englishman look like a slug from under a stone. There would be occasional film shows of Redskins and Apaches provided by the Indian contractor or the Army Kinema Corporation. If the sea was within reach, they would undoubtedly be given a day at the seaside.

One day it might be that the company commander would receive some information or have a bright idea, and the patrol leader, an officer, sergeant or corporal, would be given orders. This would take place in the operations tent in front of a great operations map covered with coloured pins and mystic symbols. However inaccurate the pins and information might be they were important, for there must be some basis for conjecture, plans and hopes. The plan would be propounded and discussed, and then the details of timings, men, transport, food and so on would be arranged.

The patrol commander would make his plan and then

probably assemble his men in the operations room where they could all see the masterpiece, the operations map. Then everyone would go away to get ready, for they would be off before dawn the next morning. Rations would be drawn and packed away in haversacks; margarine and biscuits, being heavy and of little value, tend to get left behind; while the tinned fare is usually supplemented with onions, rice and curry powder—everything, it seems, can be curried except tinned bacon. 'Muckers' decide who is to carry what of their great heap of impedimenta. Parangs are sharpened. Weapons are tested on the camp range. When the wheezy popping of the camp generator mercifully fades away and the lights go out, the patrol is soon asleep.

All too soon the engine coughs into life as the duty driver cranks it and the camp awake. The unwashed and sleepy patrol eat a quick breakfast, collect their bulging kits and stagger through the dark to the waiting trucks. As they pass the camp guardroom, every man cocks his weapon. It is cold in the trucks, as the night air whips through the thin jungle cloth, and all will be glad to get on the move when the trucks stop on the fringe of a rubber estate. The trucks turn for camp with their escorts, the sick and lame probably, alert in the rear against the danger of ambush. The patrol slips off into the breaking dawn. It is about 6.30 a.m., the invariable time of the Malayan dawn, and they can see well enough through the rubber. In the jungle it will still be dark and a halt may be necessary before they can move on. In an hour they will have covered some four hundred yards and they stop for the first halt. Everyone will be black with sweat. The patrol leader and any other leaders will check position: two heads are often better than one when navigating in the jungle. The men smoke cigarettes and pick leeches off one another; some take salt tablets. In ten minutes they are on their way again. A scout leads, generally a junior Non-Commissioned officer, with the patrol leader next. If an Iban, of whom more later, is not leading, which he will certainly do if it is a case of tracking, he will probably come next; he will cut low lianas and ensnaring 'wait-a-bit' brambles so that the over-laden signaller can have as easy a passage as possible. A bren gun will be fairly near the front in case of trouble. If it is a long march, friends will relieve the signaller of his set. The patrol leader will not have to worry about that; the men know the problem well and will solve it themselves, for in the jungle every man co-operates.

Eventually a suitable site is found for the base camp near water. At once the patrol forms a circle, packs are dropped and in silence each pair or group of men 'base up', that is, build a 'basha', a light frame of saplings over which are tied poncho capes. Attap branches are laid on the ground, a liana is erected chest high around the camp, a latrine is dug, a water-point is made. A trained patrol will do this in ten to fifteen minutes. A patrol goes out to ensure that no bandits are about. Everyone rests and 'brews up'. The medical orderly goes round tending cuts, sores and stings. Later, the evening meal is cooked by comrades together in their bashas on their 'Tommy Cookers'; most men make curry. At dusk the patrol stands to and the patrol leader issues rum. Meanwhile the evening air is filled with the astonishing chatter of myriads of insects as they embark on their ecstatic evening song. Night falls swiftly in the jungle and the patrol turns in for the tropical night's twelve long hours of darkness. One man stands sentry in the middle of the camp.

Every day patrols will go out from base to search their area. They will set forth lightly equipped, in threes and fours, moving on compass bearings through the jungle. They may cover, according to the terrain, up to four thousand yards before they turn for camp, which they should reach before 4 p.m. Most will have the sad refrain: 'Nan Tare Roger' (N.T.R. or 'Nothing to Report'). Some will have been lucky to have found a bandit resting-place, a footprint, an old camp. The signaller will then, squatting in the sweaty gloom of his low basha, start slowly tapping out the daily situation report to his mate sitting in the sunshine miles away. If there is an important message to receive, the waiting patrol leader, peering over the perspiring neck of his patient signaller, will suffer agonies as the letters slowly form into words, and then sentences, on the message pad. Sometimes a lucky patrol will be near a river or sizeable stream and then, with due precautions, all will go bathing in the evening after the day's work.

On the last morning camp is struck—nothing is left that could be of conceivable use to the bandits—and with light hearts and lighter packs the patrol starts for the open. If navigation and timing are correct, they will break from the jungle gloom to find the trucks waiting in the bright sunshine. Then, pallid and unshaven, filthy and tattered, they will be motored back to the hot sunshine and relative comfort of the company base camp. Patrols such as this were going out day after day and month after month. Most had to report 'Nan Tare Roger'; it was only the skilful, and lucky, who once in the whole three years would have the excitement and thrill of a thirty seconds' engagement with a half-seen bandit, and woe betide them if they missed!

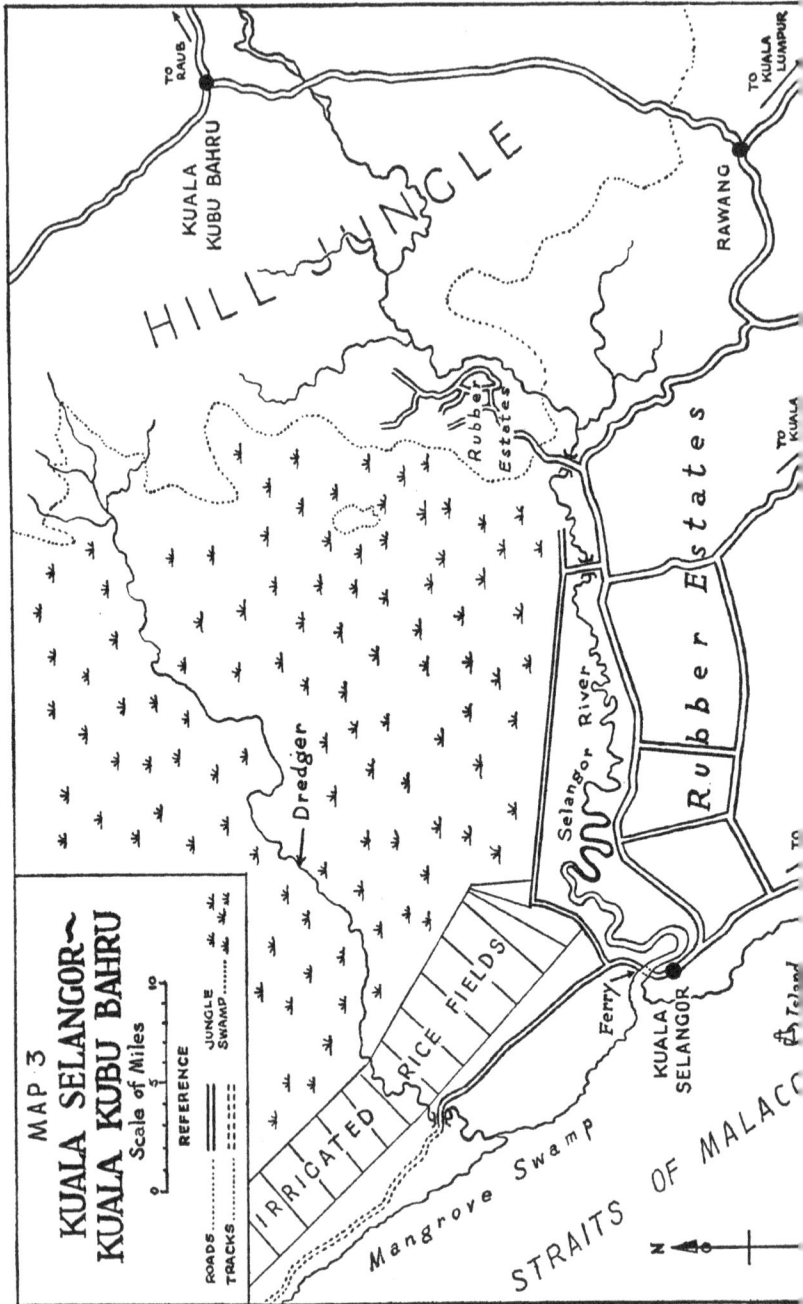

MAP 3

KUALA SELANGOR~
KUALA KUBU BAHRU

Scale of Miles

0   5   10

REFERENCE

ROADS .... ═══════
TRACKS .... ┅┅┅┅┅
JUNGLE .... ═══════
SWAMP .... ┅┅┅┅┅

TO RAUB

KUALA KUBU BAHRU

HILL JUNGLE

TO KUALA LUMPUR

RAWANG

TO KUALA

Rubber Estates

Rubber Estates

Dredger

Selangor River

TO

IRRIGATED RICE FIELDS

Ferry

KUALA SELANGOR

Mangrove Swamp

TO

Island

STRAITS OF MALACCA

N

CHAPTER FOUR

MALAYA: AROUND KUALA LUMPUR[1]

The new area – Cloak-and-dagger operations – A notable
ambush – A full-scale operation – Bandit supplies – A tragic
ambush – The Ibans – Ceremonial occasions and visits – New
tasks at Kuala Selangor and Kuala Kubu Bahru – A bandit
ambush – A chase and some successes – Helicopters – Reinforcements and National Service – Re-training – A frustrating period – Move to Pahang – List of office-holders.

WITH the successful conclusion of the operations in the North
Swamp, attention was turned to the jungle hills to the east of
Kuala Lumpur, where the second-ranking terrorist in the
Federation, Yong Kwo lived. For this operation the whole
Battalion, with the exception of A Company, left to flounder
in their swamp at Sepang, was concentrated around the
capital. D Company remained at Kajang, where their opera-
tional area in the Ulu Langat valley connected with Yong
Kwo's area and could have direct bearing on the rest of the
Battalion's activity.

It was a most difficult operation in a very troublesome
area. Kuala Lumpur was a large, sprawling and thriving city,
which could scarcely be dealt with in the same manner as
an isolated village. Chinese squatter areas, one adjoining the
Battalion's camp at Wardieburn, and all defying any attempts
at serious control, increased the difficulties, as also did a
number of tin mines on the city outskirts. Both the Chinese
squatter area at Setepak and the tin mines were known to
harbour keen Communist sympathizers, and the 'Min Yuen'
supply lines were firmly based on 'Masses' Executives' in these
two areas. Bandits were even reported to have been shopping
in Kuala Lumpur. It was certainly true that their supply lines
ran within sight of the officers' mess at Wardieburn camp.

[1] See Map Three.

The terrain for this operation was basically in the terrorists' favour. The 'Masses' Executives' lived in a semi-circle of uncontrolled squatter settlements around the eastern fringes of the city. Outside this semi-circle lay a belt, two miles or so wide, of tin mines, some disused with a waste of ten-foot-high sword-grass obstructing the view. In this belt were a few rubber estates, some in a very overgrown condition, which again obstructed the view. There was the 'new village' of Ampang inside its wire fence. There were three waterworks, around which the secondary jungle was almost impenetrable. Then, with the first broken ground, started the jungle, thick at first and then thinning and rising very steeply to considerable heights. Although the terrorists did not themselves make use of the highest hills, patrols had to go there to find this out. The hills where they lived ran from about 600 to 800 feet and were extremely steep and narrow. The Battalion's assignment was to cut the supply lines of a relatively small number of bandits, who could only be intercepted within a waste zone some two miles wide and some eight miles long: no easy task.

Because of the terrain in which the Battalion was forced to operate, many incidents took on a cloak-and-dagger aspect, in which a handful of police and a few chosen soldiers went out on an attempted *coup-de-main* in a squatter village. Some of these were successful. Often areas were denied to the Battalion by Special Branch. This meant that Special Branch either hoped to bring off something on their own, or that they were afraid that the soldiery might upset some of their informers. This was a difficult situation and was a frequent cause of friction. The operation was, by and large, a frustrating period. The soldiers patently felt that they were not getting anywhere, and superior headquarters, getting restive at the lack of results, tended to interfere. Before long there was a considerable feeling of strain at all levels. This was heightened when a few natives, breaking curfew regulations, were mistaken by ambush parties for terrorists and shot; this only served to accentuate the difficulties of trying to operate as soldiers on the outskirts of a great and busy city.

To illustrate further the difficulties of this area for soldiers, the Nam Koon Kongsi is perhaps a good example. Each tin mine had a Kongsi, a large building in which the Chinese labourers and their families lived a strange communal existence. The Nam Koon Kongsi was known to support the terrorists; they were keen 'Masses' Executives' and a constant flow of supplies emanated from this source. This was well known to Special Branch and, as it was not many hundred yards from the officers' mess at Wardieburn, one might have supposed that its control was no great problem. It could, of course, have been closed down, but this was quite unacceptable to the Malayan economy. The bandits had to be physically intercepted and destroyed. Easier said than done.

It was known that a small boy would climb a certain tree, adjacent to the Kongsi and in sight of the officers' mess, if the coast, from the terrorists' point of view, was clear. If Security Forces were about, he would not climb the tree and the bandit supply party, who were watching from the nearby jungle, would not venture forth. Innumerable stratagems were employed to no avail. Lieutenant-Colonel Brind and his Intelligence Officer, Lieutenant J. H. F. Mackie, disguised themselves as electricians inspecting the overhead cables. Other officers went out on reconnaissances in the guise of shooting parties after duck or pig. Although a few duck were doubtless killed in this way, it was many months before there was any success against the bandits. Eventually, however, as is recounted later, Lieutenant A. F. Raikes, employing novel tactics for an impossible military problem, succeeded. Meanwhile, an intractable situation defied even unconventional military tactics.

But major success came very near. On 6 September 1953 Sergeant Lee, with a patrol of Ibans, moving along a jungle trail, became aware that it had been used that very day. Moving carefully, they spotted a bandit pack hidden under some bamboo off the track. The sergeant concluded that its owner was likely to return for it pretty soon and promptly set an ambush. They were hardly in position before four terrorists were seen coming down the track. They opened fire on the two most heavily armed men. One was killed instantly, the other after a short chase. The two others got away. Later investigation proved the two dead men to be Yong Kwo's bodyguard and that he himself was the third member of the party and only owed his life to being less heavily armed than his guards. It was not until later that it became generally known that, the higher the rank of a bandit, the more lightly armed was he likely to be. Chinese Communist leaders, being rather old-fashionedly autocratic in their ideas, liked to go about armed with pistols. Yong Kwo seemed to have a charmed life and was not in fact killed until 1957 by the Rifle Brigade.

It was now decided to launch a full-scale operation against Yong Kwo and his supporting groups. For this, a battalion of Gurkhas as well as the whole of the 1st Battalion were deployed. Police and administrators tightened up their controls. A Company returned to the Battalion from Sepang and was stationed at Ampang. The broad plan was that the Gurkhas, seasoned jungle fighters with a great record, should patrol in the jungle for up to fourteen days at a time, while the Battalion controlled the jungle fringes and in particular tried to prevent food getting into the jungle.

The operation started propitiously with a surrender in the Ulu Langat area. Lieutenant D. R. Goddard killed another terrorist in an ambush in the middle of a terrific electric storm. A B Company ambush, opening up at long range at night, recovered a pack belonging to a member of Yong Kwo's printing press. These occurred at the turn of the year 1953–4. Nothing then happened until March 1954, when a bandit surrendered to the filter pump watchman at the Headquarters of the Malayan Command, which was sited on a comfortable hill in the middle of the Battalion's ambush positions. This at least encouraged Headquarters. In June two more surrendered as a result of an action with a police unit. So, although things were dragging on interminably with little tangible to show for all the work, there was some progress. The Gurkhas had long been sent elsewhere, amazed at the utter lack of anything to show for their all-out efforts.

Unfortunately opportunities were missed that could be ill afforded. Support Company failed to get two terrorists in a night ambush. An A Company patrol, under a particularly experienced patrol leader, failed in a very difficult attack on a camp in thick secondary jungle not eight hundred yards from the company permanent base at Ampang. On the other hand, Lieutenant A. F. Raikes, using mobile night patrol tactics in the scrub not very far from the officers' mess at Wardieburn Camp, killed two important bandits. Later the head of the Setapak 'Min Yuen' branch surrendered. As a result of this, and with his help, vast supplies of bandit food were recovered from the jungle, so that it seemed as if Yong Kwo's supply organization might be broken.

So far, much has been made of killing or capturing terrorists. As has been seen, this occurred remarkably rarely. Indeed, there must have been many hundreds of men in the Battalion who never saw one in the wild. But there were other actions in the jungle that could be almost as important as actual killing. The finding and destroying of camps was most important, as this made the bandits move, and moving bandits were easier to kill than stationary ones. Then to find and remove a food dump was a major gain; it might contain anything: drums of rice, bottles of oil, sauces, salt, sugar, tapioca, clothes and waterproof material, paper, ink and printing matter. Even an unsuccessful ambush could have felicitous results: the bandits would have to open a new route, a rendezvous might have to be changed, packs, weapons and food supplies might well be jettisoned in their flight. This would all add up.

One particularly successful coup, which has a bearing on food supplies, was brought off by the resourcefulness of Corporal Cridge. He was on his way out of the jungle at the end of a patrol, when he encountered a logging lorry on its way in. He searched it and found food concealed in the back. When questioned, the driver admitted that he was taking it to a bandit rendezvous and was forced to take the whole patrol with him to the hiding place. Here Corporal Cridge laid an ambush, placing the Chinaman between the Iban and another N.C.O. In due course the terrorists appeared but, at the crucial moment, the driver broke free and ran forward shouting. He was shot dead in the ensuing firing and the bandits got away. Nonetheless the effects of this would be far-reaching, for the terrorists would be forced to find and organize a new supply line, which would certainly be difficult, if not dangerous.

Another source of bandit food supply were jungle cultivation areas. Here they grew sweet potatoes and tapioca. Patrols spent many hours locating and destroying them. Auster aircraft were useful in spotting them and could be used to guide patrols to them. Attempts were made to destroy the crops chemically by spraying them on the ground, or from the air by helicopters, but, tedious though it was, destruction by hand was generally more reliable.

There was one very tragic accident during this time. Late one night the Head of Special Branch asked for a small party to assist in a *coup-de-main* in a particularly notorious area, and decided to lead the raid himself. Lieutenant J. H. F. Mackie, the Intelligence officer, and Lieutenant D. R. Goddard went along with a few men. A plan was made between the police and the soldiers, and the ambush, under Goddard, was set behind a house. The plan was that the police should demand entry at the front of the house and that the terrorists, fleeing by the back, would be shot down. Unfortunately, for some reason never elucidated, having failed to get any response at the front of the house, the police party went round to the rear. They were instantly shot. The Head of Special Branch died of his wounds and Mackie was eventually invalided out of the army. It was a tragic accident. No blame could be attached to anyone, but it did help to show how difficult for soldiers were these clandestine operations. Yet to extirpate terrorists from the squatter areas around Kuala Lumpur these sort of operations were essential.

Mention has been made of the Ibans, or Sarawak Rangers, from Borneo. They knew all about the jungle and were expert trackers: their skill was uncanny, when tracking, and when the scent was hot, they went faster than any hunting dog. These men lived up the great rivers of North Borneo, to a point barely penetrated by civilization, some living over two hundred miles inland. Their life was a communal one, each village living in one 'Long House': a long wooden building normally raised on stilts at the river's edge. Here each family occupied one room and the life of the village took place on the verandah running the length of the building or in the open space in front of it. They were an essentially friendly and hospitable race, whose most noticeable characteristic was cheerfulness, which rapidly endeared them to the soldiers. They were recruited by British officers in Borneo where there was considerable competition to enlist for overseas service and acquire Chinese heads. Lieutenant R. W. Houghton, Lieutenant H. Atkinson and Lieutenant J. Bentz all visited Borneo, either for recruiting purposes or to look after their men on the journey, and travelled far up-country, living in the village 'Long Houses'.

The Ibans were used for two purposes in Malaya: as trackers, and as a platoon with English officers and Non-Commissioned officers. The trackers normally worked in pairs and were allotted to a particular platoon of soldiers, with whom they quickly became firm friends and trusted companions in the jungle. A pair of good trackers could be of immense value to a patrol leader, but of course some were less skilful than others. Apart from their skill as trackers, they were experts at living in the jungle and the men rapidly picked up jungle lore from them. The soldiers, however, did not copy them when it came to catching and cooking snakes, iguanas and tortoises. They were surprisingly poor marksmen, being happiest when armed with a shot-gun, and more than one bandit owed his life to an Iban, leading a patrol and busy tracking, missing his man. The patrol leader, just behind him, and relying on his tracker for a moment too long, would be unable to fire or even see the target.

They were mostly illiterate and, when in camp, would happily while away the time making fishing or hunting traps, making parangs or having more charms tattooed on their nut-brown bodies. Their religion, apparently animist, sometimes led them to express disapproval of a patrol on the grounds of the omens being inauspicious. But they were absolutely honest, straightforward and truthful; the only occasions on which they might show annoyance was when they suspected that they had been told a lie. Most of them picked up a few essential phrases of English and communicating with them was never a problem.

The Iban platoon was quite a separate entity and operated in exactly the same way as a British platoon, but could be expected to move through the jungle faster and cover greater distances. They were also poor shots, even after a lot of practice, and it was disappointing that this platoon did not have more kills to its credit: perhaps ill-luck outweighed its obvious skill, courage and competence. In fact it was probably a mistake to form these platoons; the men would have been, by and large, more usefully dispersed as trackers throughout the Battalion. This platoon was commanded most of the time by Lieutenant R. W. Houghton with Sergeant Lee and Corporals Ballantyne, Abernathy and Mellhuish as Non-Commissioned officers. They all spoke some Malay.

In addition to the Ibans for tracking, there were also patrol and tracker dogs. The former were rarely of much use. They were a liability in any swamp as they had to be carried and were often unable to keep up in rough country. Despite the innumerable times that they were taken on patrol, the results were most disappointing. This was a pity and, indeed, a waste, for the dog-handlers were always specially selected men, who would probably have been more valuable without the encumbrance of their dogs. Each dog-handler had to carry his dog's rations on patrol, which was quite an addition to the weight on his back. Tracker dogs, however, had their uses and were sometimes employed to follow up a wounded terrorist and occasionally were able to put a patrol on the bandit's trail.

Each company had three interpreters, normally Chinese from Malacca or Penang, but sometimes Tamils. These were used to interpret when a patrol had to take a surrendered bandit out with them. Some were resolute, tough and admirable men, others were quite unreliable, which was dangerous for they could be of immense help to a patrol leader by winning the confidence of the ex-bandit. One of the terrorists' conceits was that they talked high Chinese Mandarin, but this was rarely so and the interpreter had first to wean the surrendered bandit from this absurdity. Then he had to cajole and slowly extract information that would be of use to the patrol leader. This was not easy, for the average ex-bandit would begin to have obvious doubts and fears, as he led the patrol ever nearer to his late comrades. They were important members of most patrols.

Life in Malaya was not all 'jungle bashing', particularly when the Battalion was based on Kuala Lumpur, for distinguished visitors to the capital had to be received with due ceremony and generally wanted to visit the troops. The Battalion, being the nearest unit, was frequently involved in their reception. At the Malayan Coronation Parade on 2 June 1953 the Battalion provided the Guard of Honour for the High Commissioner, Sir Gerald Templer. Both Guard and the Band and Bugles were dressed for the first time in the new white Number Three Dress. Another Guard of Honour was found by the Battalion for the farewell parade for General Templer. Distinguished visitors included Adlai Stevenson, the twice defeated Democrat candidate for the White House, who went to Kajang to talk with the men of D Company. His opponent and fellow countryman, Vice-President Nixon, also visited D Company. Major Ogilvie had the skill and good fortune to be able to produce a bandit who had that very moment surrendered. Whether the Communist terrorist was impressed by the fact that almost his first contact with the free world was a member of the United States Government will never be known. Neither will it ever be known what impact this meeting may have had on the member of an avowedly anti-colonial administration. There were countless other visitors such as French and American officers on tour, American and Australian journalists—who wrote alarming descriptions of the jungle Hell—an Australian scientist, a professor of hygiene, Royal Air Force officers and Royal Naval midshipmen. The Colonel of the Regiment, in his capacity of Chief of the Imperial General Staff, took advantage of a world tour to visit the Battalion, dining with the officers and visiting the sergeants. The Minister of Defence, Duncan Sandys, also visited the Battalion and was shown a display of jungle equipment.

On 10 June 1954 there was a complete re-distribution of troops in the State of Selangor, which resulted in the Battalion becoming responsible for the whole state. Previously there had been three battalions engaged there. As a result of this A Company was moved to Kuala Selangor, where they became responsible for the largest jungle swamp in Malaya and the new rice-growing district between the jungle and the coast. C Company moved to Kuala Kubu Bahru to chase a particularly unpleasant bandit with a long record of murder and crime, called Heap Theong. D Company remained at Kajang and continued to look after their previous area. B Company remained at Wardieburn Camp outside Kuala Lumpur with duties around the capital.

A and C Companies were about fifty miles apart and had some 500 square miles each to look after and, although at first sight it did not appear likely that operations in either of their areas could have any effect on the other, this was soon disproved. The operational area, apart from its immensity, was extremely difficult. Inland from the coastal mangrove swamps lay the rice fields, a rectangular area of roughly a hundred square miles intersected by irrigation channels.

There were no proper roads, and patrols travelled to the jungle in jeeps and trailers—a practice that was both comic and dangerous. This journey took two hours from A Company base. There were several Chinese villages, whose unfortunate inhabitants were being terrorized into providing food and money; judicious murders saw to it that this would continue. The bandits lived across the main canal that divided the jungle from cultivation. The police had the unpleasant task of patrolling the rice fields; unpleasant, because the narrow paths along the irrigation channels had been allowed to become dangerously overgrown. The jungle was swamp and the going desperate. In the middle of the swamp lay a dredger, engaged in clearing the sluggish river that ran otherwise unseen through it. Here lived a party of police and wood-cutters. Periodically the water level at the dredger fell so low that the river became unnavigable and these men were marooned. Theirs was an unenviable position even with no terrorists about.

Almost immediately after A Company's arrival at Kuala Selangor a serious incident occurred. A police patrol was ambushed on the main canal by a party of about forty bandits. The Malay policemen quickly discharged all their ammunition and then had their weapons ignominiously removed by the terrorists. This was a serious blow to police morale and a dangerous increase of arms to the bandits. The leader of this bandit ambush party was none other than Heap Theong, who was supposed to be in C Company's area at Kuala Kubu Bahru.

The pursuit started at dawn the following day under Sergeant Cox. It was a testing and dangerous task, for the terrorists, flushed with victory and new weapons, might well arrange to ambush their pursuers. Bandits could move faster in the swamp than soldiers and laid false trails that had to be investigated. Lincoln bombers were used to drop bombs ahead of the bandits in an attempt to head them off. But inevitably the pursuers fell behind, being further delayed by the need for supplies being dropped to them. Owing to the

Company's recent arrival in the area, there were as yet no cleared dropping zones for the Valetta aircraft, and as there was obviously no time to stop and make them, supplies had to be dropped by free-drop from Auster aircraft—a perilous game for those at the receiving end.

Meanwhile, another platoon had been helicoptered to the dredger, partly to bolster up the police in case they too should be attacked, and partly to try to intercept the bandits who were believed to have a track nearby. C Company were also alerted, for it was probable that Heap Theong would make his way back to his normal area. Major P. Haigh laid his plans with great skill, and ambushes were set on likely terrorist routes along the high ridges that led towards Kuala Kubu Bahru. On 25 June 1954 a party of bandits walked into one such ambush party commanded by Lance-Corporal Dipper, who shot the leading man dead. Heap Theong was in the party and got away unscathed. This same corporal was successful again a few days later, when he killed a second terrorist from another ambush position. Sergeant Bone accounted for one more and Lieutenant T. W. M. Hustler attacked a camp, killing another. So Major Haigh's plan for the reception of Heap Theong had not been without satisfactory results.

Back in Kuala Selangor, Sergeant Cox's patrol had had to be recalled, many of his young soldiers being utterly exhausted by the rigours of their chase. Meanwhile additional troops were rushed into the area: a Gurkha company, a squadron of Malays of the Royal Air Force Regiment, the Iban Platoon and finally D Company from Kajang. But, in the short time left before the Battalion was due to be taken off jungle operations for re-training, little could be either expected or achieved. The only success was that of Corporal Melluish of the Ibans, who surprised some terrorists around a water-hole, and luckily killed the bandit sentry who was just about to shoot an Iban corporal. He recovered one of the rifles taken from the police in the bandit ambush.

Helicopters were now much more prolific, manned by

both the Royal Air Force and the Royal Navy, and were being put to increasingly good use by the soldiers. Previously it had been almost impossible to obtain them, although occasional use had been made of them for spraying crops, taking the mortars into the jungle and once for an attempted *coup-de-main* on a terrorist hide-out. Their value was enormous in saving both time and sweat. At Kuala Selangor, for instance, it might have taken three days for a patrol to reach the dredger on foot; a whole platoon was carried there in about half an hour by one helicopter. Often the helicopter could not touch down owing to the state of the ground, and then the men swarmed up and down a knotted rope. On one such occasion, owing to a misunderstanding with the pilot, a man was still on the rope when the helicopter flew off; a fifteen-mile flight over virgin jungle on the end of a rope was not a particularly amusing experience for this man, who was lucky to have had the strength to hang on. From now on helicopters were to play an ever-increasingly important part in all operations and it became standard practice, on arrival in a new area, for helicopter landing zones to be made deep in the jungle as soon as possible, as well as dropping-zones for Valetta aircraft with supplies. The Pioneer Platoon was used to help in blowing down the jungle giants with explosives. Another aspect of their use was the surprise factor; the terrorists never knew whether helicopters overhead meant troops being taken in or out of the jungle, whether they were being changed over or, indeed, whether the aircraft was merely evacuating a sick man. This last role was of immense value to commanders in the jungle, for they knew that if they had a seriously ill man on their hands, he would be in hospital in a matter of minutes providing they could get him to a landing zone. It was a great uplift to morale and must have saved many lives.

The Battalion was now due to be taken off all operational duties for two months, and this is a good point at which to review the man-power problem in Malaya with special reference to National Service; for during this period, when the

Battalion was stretched to its utmost, with commitments over the whole of Selangor, its strength had fallen alarmingly. All companies were affected and some were operating with platoons reduced in strength to ten men. Superior Headquarters might look at their operational maps, where bright pins showed platoons engaged on certain tasks, but they were probably quite unaware that some of the pins represented a numerically derisory military force.

The problem presented by the constant turn-over of National Servicemen was nothing new but neither in England nor in Germany had it been so pressing or so apparent. For one thing, the men had not taken so long to travel to and fro and, more important, there was less urgency in peace-time manœuvres. Now they were required for war in a far distant land. The recruit, after his ten weeks' training at the Depot, his embarkation leave, and a four to five weeks' journey by troopship could not at once be sent out on patrol. On arrival, he joined Support Company for a period of advanced training in his new weapons, in jungle skills and for acclimitization. During this period the instructors were on the look-out for potential leaders, for clerks and for signallers, of which there was a permanent shortage and for which, owing to sadly low educational standards, few were initially fitted.

Those selected for specialist training then went on their courses which, in the case of signallers for instance, might require another two months before they could join a patrol. Newly arrived officers and many Non-Commissioned officers were sent to the Jungle Training Centre at Kota Tinggi to learn their new trade. As the efficiency or otherwise, of a patrol was in direct relation to the skill and competence of its leader, it was important that they should be as adequately grounded as possible before going into the jungle. This was best done by the experts at the Training Centre.

It is interesting to note some figures relating to the turn-over. During the first eighteen months in Malaya thirty-three officers, of whom fourteen were National Servicemen, were posted to the Battalion and it lost thirty-two, nine of them National Servicemen; 812 Other Ranks arrived and 845 left: a loss of over thirty. And all the time there were up to a hundred men somewhere in the 'pipeline' between the Depot and the Battalion, some coming, some going and some under advanced training. Owing to the vagaries of troopship sailings, some men might have to leave their rifle companies up to six or seven weeks before they were officially due at the Depot for their release. A few drafts arrived by air, but this great saving in time was often offset by the too sudden change of climate, which retarded their acclimatization.

One of the sad things from the Battalion's point of view was that the average National Serviceman was just about at his most valuable when he fell due to go home; had he stayed, he would have made an admirable leader. In his place came a novice, and the whole process started again. All the same these National Servicemen filled the majority of junior leader ranks: ninety per cent of the lance-corporals were always National Servicemen and at least half the corporals: at least one became a sergeant. In fact it is true to say that the average National Serviceman was of superior calibre to his Regular counterpart, which is no surprise at a time of full employment. They had, of course, one big advantage over the Regular: that of doing a worthwhile job, albeit in foul conditions, for a definitely limited period. The Regular was committed to the same job for a full three years—and three years of 'jungle bashing' was a long time.

One of the by-products of National Service was the fact that the Orderly Room and Quartermaster's staffs became greatly inflated. This was for two reasons: one was that the constant turn-over of men produced more paper work in the form of filling in documents and handing equipment in and out; the other was that most clerks had an understudy waiting to replace the present incumbent when he was released. On top of this, the Quartermaster's departments were mostly, at the behest of the Command Secretaries, on a peace-time accounting system; when it is realized that one sergeant wore out fifty-three pairs of jungle boots in his three years, the prodigious amount of paper work involved can be appreciated.

No one would wish to, nor could, belittle the value of National Servicemen in Malaya, or elsewhere. It is true that they caused more work, produced wasteful overheads, resulted in periodic inefficiencies and many headaches for the Regular cadre; but this cross-section of the nation were splendid and enthusiastic men who helped to make a happy and successful battalion. The National Service officers, with their Regular Sergeants at their elbows, were particularly successful leaders. Military crime was practically non-existent, so willingly did all work together. And of course the National Servicemen paid the price, as did the others, of casualties: some killed in action, or as a result of lamentable accidents and others dying through illness.

The all-Regular army of the future will be a more economical and more efficient force, like its predecessors of 1914 and 1939; but the living contact with the nation, in the form of the never-ending flow of young men from civilian life, will be a very real loss that perhaps even efficiency will not outweigh. Since the war, and thanks to National Service, the Regiment and the County have grown ever closer, as was so abundantly proved by the welcome given to the Regiment at Taunton and Wells when the Battalion returned, and it seems likely that this powerful source of good-will may diminish when National Service ends.

On 12 August 1954 the whole Battalion assembled at Wardieburn Camp, outside Kuala Lumpur, where it was to spend two months, relieved of all jungle tasks, for what was known as re-training. Each British battalion in Malaya was given these two months off operations once in the middle of its three years' tour. This was partly to allow it to get together again as a battalion, partly as a change and rest, and partly to carry out essential military tasks that could not be done so long as the battalion was split up in company detachments all over the country.

During this period companies fired their range courses and had a week at the seaside at Seginting where there was an excellent sandy bathing beach. Brigadier C. S. Howard, the late commanding officer, carried out the annual administrative inspection. A certain amount of ceremonial drill was performed in preparation for an inspection by the Gurkha Divisional Commander, Major-General L. E. C. M. Perowne. A Guard of Honour was found for the visit of Antony Head, the Secretary of State for War, who also paid a visit to the Battalion. And of course an immense amount of games and sports were organized between companies, who had for so long been almost unable to compete against one another, and resulted in a heartening revival of the battalion spirit. Battalion teams were also able to take the field again at full strength. Of these perhaps the most notable was the soccer team which, under the direction of Major Smart and Regimental Sergeant-Major Bartlett, reached an unusually high standard of excellence and had a series of successful seasons while the Battalion was in Malaya.

It is appropriate here to mention the Somerset Comforts Fund. While the Battalion was in Malaya, a fund to provide comforts for the men had been formed in the County and, as a result of the generosity of the people of Somerset, there was a constant flow of both money and gifts. This materially helped to ease the lot of the men and was certainly much appreciated.

On 12 October 1954 the Battalion returned to jungle operations. Again it was responsible for the whole of the State of Selangor. But in view of the fact that it was now known that the Battalion was to move to the State of Pahang for a completely new operation in December, little could be expected in the short time available. No long-term projects could be undertaken and companies operated in their new areas on a very temporary basis. B and D Companies were made responsible for the South Swamp around Sepang, C Company returned to Kuala Kubu Bahru, and A Company were given odd jobs around the capital. There was one interesting attempt to try to bomb a terrorist camp, but it was unsuccessful. Lieutenant J. O. C. Crawford carried out a successful night ambush, killing two bandits. Otherwise there were no successes. There were insufficient troops, the area was too vast, there was no co-ordinated plan with the police and administrators, and there was inadequate time in which to get to grips with the problems. It was with considerable relief that the Battalion moved over the mountainous central ridge into the State of Pahang. It now had from 1 December 1954 until September 1955 to set about its new tasks in its new area.

The following were the principal office-holders during the period in Selangor:

Commanding Officer .	Lieutenant-Colonel J. L. Brind, D.S.O.
Second-in-command .	Major V. S. Baily
Adjutant . . .	Captain C. D. C. Frith
Quartermaster . .	Captain T. Meredith, M.B.E.
R.S.M. . . .	R.S.M. K. E. Bartlett
Headquarter Company	Major T. M. Braithwaite, M.C. C.S.M. E. W. Broadbent
A Company . .	Major K. J. Whitehead, M.C. C.S.M. E. A. Giles, M.M.
B Company . .	Major R. J. Stevens C.S.M. R. Harton (K.S.L.I.)
C Company . .	Major P. Haigh C.S.M. A. J. Longney
D Company . .	Captain T. Lock (Major C. W. E. Satterthwaite took over in August) C.S.M. J. Piercey, M.M. (K.O.Y.L.I.)
Support Company .	Major H. McLean C.S.M. G. King
Bandmaster . .	Bandmaster W. H. Moore, A.R.C.M.

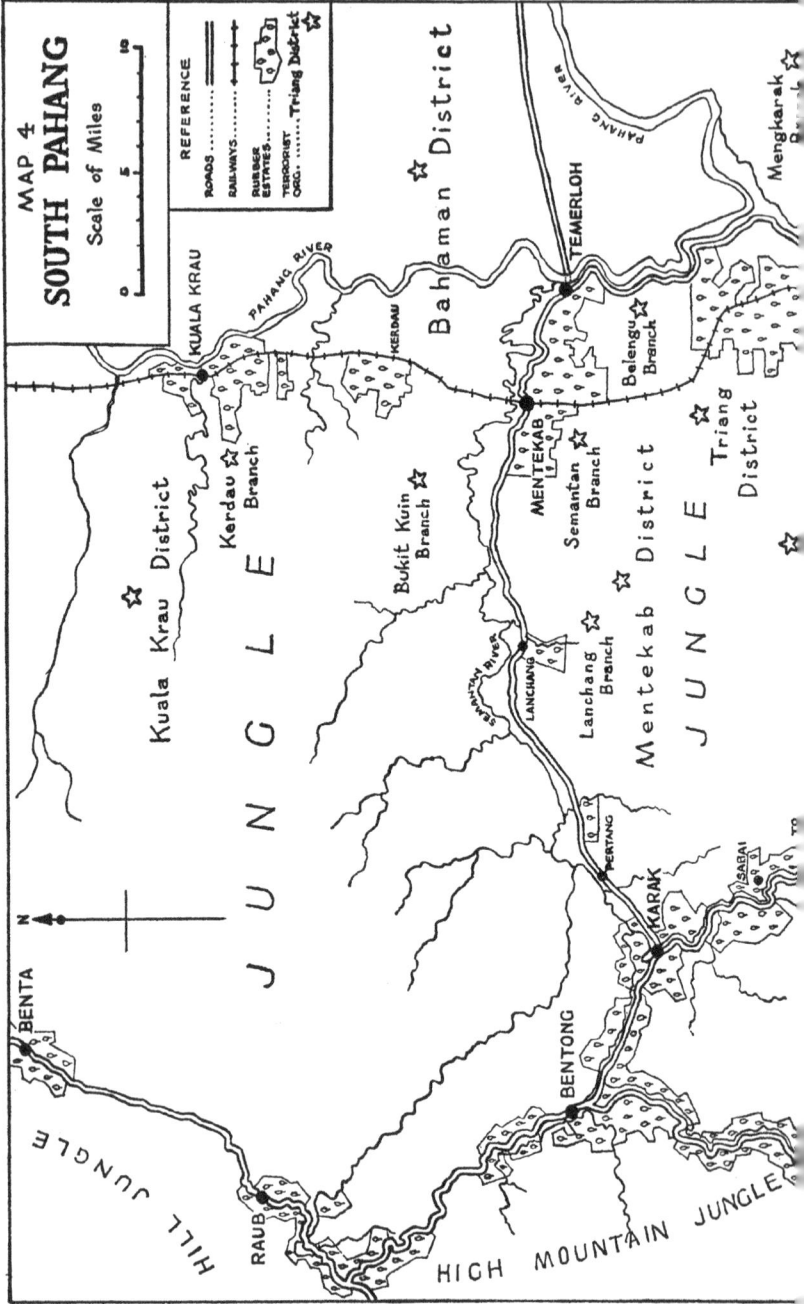

MAP 4
SOUTH PAHANG

Scale of Miles

0   5   10

REFERENCE

ROADS ....
RAILWAYS ....
RUBBER
ESTATES ....
TERRORIST
ORG. .... Triang District

BENTA

HILL JUNGLE

RAUB

HIGH MOUNTAIN JUNGLE

BENTONG

KARAK

PERTANG

SABAI

TO

LANCHANG

Lanchang
Branch

SEMANTAN RIVER

Bukit Kuin
Branch

Kerdau
Branch

KUALA KRAU

PAHANG RIVER

KERDAU

Kuala Krau District

JUNGLE

N

Mentekab District

Semantan
Branch

MENTEKAB

Belengu
Branch

Bahaman District

TEMERLOH

PAHANG RIVER

JUNGLE

Triang
District

Mengkarak
Branch

CHAPTER FIVE

MALAYA: PAHANG[1]

The new area – The new terrorists – The monsoon – The
Chinese New Year camp – Kuala Krau operations – Casualties – The 'Loop' – Lieutenant-Colonel V. S. Baily in command – Re-deployment to Raub and Benta – Successes – A
successful chase – An example of co-operation – Cultivation
areas and the Sakai – A skilful patrol – Final successes –
Amnesty – Visitors – Relaxations – Problems of command –
Final assessment of tour – Singapore and return to England –
Taunton reception – Plymouth – List of office-holders.

THE area allotted for the Battalion's operations in Pahang
was very different to the one it had left. Although it was even
vaster, it was more compact. Ninety-nine per cent was jungle
and it was largely uninhabited. The few rubber estates were
widely scattered. Apart from the endless jungle, the most
noticeable thing was the rudimentary nature of the communications. There was but one road that ran laterally across the
area from Bentong to Temerloh. A primitive, single-track
railway ran north and south on the east of the area, through
which also flowed the mighty Pahang River. This railway line
was the only means of access to many of the rubber estates.
The river was used by the Malays to get to their villages.
Many of the tributaries of the Pahang River were larger than
any English river and were the only means of access to many
villages sited on them. It was not a mountainous area but one
of gently rolling, jungle-clad hills with sizeable swamps in the
declivities.

This new operational area had not been under much pressure from the Security Forces for some time and the local
bandits had become accustomed to having things very much

[1] See Map Four.

their own way, moving about and collecting supplies, food and money much as they pleased. They were known to have accumulated a fairly large reserve food supply in deep jungle dumps. They were numerous, well organized and well armed. The brains behind their organization was the South Pahang Regional Bureau supported by its printing press, the Battle News Press. It had District organizations based on Mentekab, Menchis and Triang. There was also another District of an unusual character called Bahaman: unusual, because it was entirely composed of Malay bandits. Under these Districts were thriving 'Min Yuen' Branches based on most villages. There were ample 'Masses' Executives' on which to rely for supplies in these villages. Also in this Region was the notorious Number Thirty-two Platoon, which had been responsible for the assassination of the High Commissioner, Sir Henry Gurney. The grand total was something over a hundred.

The operation was initially conducted by the 6th Malay Regiment in the Triang area, and by the Battalion in the Mentekab area. Extra police arrived in large numbers and restrictions of movement and food were progressively enforced as the operation gathered momentum. The north-west monsoon broke as the Battalion arrived, and conditions in the jungle became not only dangerous but well-nigh impossible. Small streams filled from the main rivers and started to flow uphill to the utter confusion of patrol leaders. Meanwhile Temerloh town was flooded by the rising of the Pahang River, and B Company, who were stationed there, had first of all, with the help of two amphibious D.U.K.W.s, to run supplies for the civilians through the floods from Mentekab. All this rather held up the start of the new operation.

D Company were based on a hill-top at Sabai with responsibility for the Menchis bandits. A Company were at Pertang with responsibility for the Lanchang Branch of the Mentekab District. C Company were at Temerloh with their target the Semantan Branch. At Temerloh were also B Company, responsible for the Belengu Branch initially, but later

62

to be sent after the Malay Bandits of the Bahaman District, who lived on the east side of the Pahang River where it formed a great loop. Lieutenant-Colonel Brind set up a Tactical Headquarters at Temerloh, while Main Headquarters and Support Company were at the other end of the Battalion area at Bentong.

One of the first steps, after the floods receded, was to construct helicopter landing-zones in deep jungle, which were later to pay immense dividends. As the operation widened, new landing-places had constantly to be made, but these efforts were never wasted. Right from the start great use was made of air support in all its available forms. Austers were used for reconnaissance and occasionally for free-dropping of supplies. Valetta supply drops were an almost daily occurrence, delivering to patrols anything from rations, clothes and medical supplies to such 'comforts' as whisky. In view of the vastness of the area and the primitive character of the communications, patrols tended to be out longer than had been normal in Selangor, so that providing extra supplies during a patrol became both more necessary and more common. Once landing zones had been made, helicopters were used almost daily for taking patrols in and out of the jungle and for evacuating casualties.

After one or two unsuccessful actions—a long and most difficult ambush on the Pahang River by Lieutenant B. M. Lane: an attack on a camp by Lieutenant S. J. Charkham: an abortive patrol by Major R. J. Stevens to a camp that had just been evacuated (the villagers had seen the patrol and warning had been passed to the terrorists): Major P. Haigh brought off the most spectacular action that the Battalion achieved during its three years in Malaya.

It occurred on the Chinese New Year's Day, 23 January 1955. Major Haigh and his batman Davis were carrying out routine reconnaissance patrols with a section of Ibans under Corporal Ballantyne. On the fourth day, the morning patrols had just been sent out, when a party of Ibans were fired on. Haigh, Ballantyne and Davis ran at once to the sound of the firing and soon came themselves under fire. These three, joined by the Ibans, pressed forward into the attack, dodging behind the trees as they closed with the enemy. There was a fierce ten minutes' battle, in which the bandits fired all they had got including several automatics; then they fled. Behind them they left three dead and one wounded who was captured. From identification of the dead and from valuable documents found in the camp it was substantiated that this had been an important meeting of all the branches of the Mentekab District with probably men from Thirty-two Platoon as well. There had been at least thirty terrorists in the camp, all well armed and with a light machine-gun and several automatics. It was a tremendously important, indeed brilliant, action by this small patrol. Major P. Haigh was awarded the Military Cross and Corporal J. L. F. Ballantyne and Private F. G. Davis were each awarded the Military Medal.

It is interesting to read the report that the bandits wrote on this engagement:

> That day we were attacked by more than one hundred British soldiers. They discovered us a few days before but waited until New Year's Eve and then attacked. We were besieged from not less than five directions: from the East, North-East, North and North-West. From the East the strength of the soldiers was the strongest and they took up position behind Kiew's position. Kiew was fired on by the enemy from the sentry position. Loy and others were shot not far from Ah Pow's position. Ching, Tai and Cheong were killed and Kiew was seriously wounded and captured. Everything was lost including the 'secret store'. Kiew is recovering from her wounds and her attitude is reported to be firm at present.
>
> We killed seven enemy British soldiers, including a Section leader who was seriously wounded and died later of wounds in Kuala Lipis Hospital.

It was now considered probable that Number Thirty-two Platoon had moved north to the Kuala Krau District. The

6th Malay Regiment, operating near Triang, reported that they could find no signs of them to the south. This, coupled with other reports, pointed to their being north of the Semantan River and attention was therefore turned to this new area. It was a difficult area to get at, as the only direct access was by the single-line railway; patrols had to be dropped off from an armoured rail-car, which complicated free movement enormously and often delayed operations which had to wait for the line to be free. It was also possible to approach the area by the Semantan river in Malay canoes with three days' subsequent walking. Helicopter landing-zones had therefore high priority. One platoon, bent on such a venture, were crossing a swollen river by a fallen tree-trunk when Private Howells fell in fully equipped. Corporal Perry of the Pioneer Platoon dived in and rescued him. He was officially commended for his gallantry.

In the Kuala Krau area Lieutenant E. G. Longman undertook two very long and arduous patrols. For the first he was given a surrendered terrorist, who was prepared to lead the patrol back to kill his two late comrades. They walked for five days, the bandit saying every day that he was lost. Eventually the platoon had very nearly walked the length of the jungle, and were on the point of coming out again, having covered some seventy thousand yards. Here Private Pollard and Longman came suddenly face to face with two bandits whom they shot dead. Surprisingly enough, they were the surrendered man's friends. His only reaction was to ask if he could have one of the dead men's spectacles.

On his next patrol Longman was making a landing-zone in very deep jungle. A local security patrol, moving along a river bank, was suddenly fired on by unseen foes and Private Bennet was killed outright. The patrol, under Lance-Corporal West, fired back into the undergrowth and attacked. The bandits fled leaving behind them several weeks' supply of rice. Despite the regrettable death of Bennet, it was otherwise a major stroke of good fortune, for these men were engaged in moving Thirty-two Platoon's reserve rations, which showed that they were already short of food—and they had now lost their reserve.

Other sad casualties occurred at this time. Corporal Shaw was shot by terrorists disguised as Security Forces. During the brief moment of uncertainty, when the two parties saw one another and identity was doubtful, the bandits fired, killing the corporal instantly. Lieutenant B. B. Heath, in charge of one patrol, clashed accidentally with another from his own platoon and in the ensuing fire fight was shot, dying later of his wounds. Sergeant Hanlon, in charge of a civilian food convoy, was killed in an ambush by Number Three Platoon M.R.L.A. from the neighbouring State of Negri Sembilan. Private Broomfield, driving the rear escorting vehicle, managed to drive to the head of the column and drive off the bandits; a very courageous action. An acrimonious discussion followed this tragic ambush between the officials of Pahang and Negri Sembilan: the former complaining that Negri Sembilan should look after their own bandits and not let them stray, and the latter trying to deny that they owned them. In fact this ambush was proved to have been prepared and rehearsed by Number Three Platoon over quite a long period.

The Bahaman District proved a most stubborn area with which to cope, and B Company had a series of great disappointments in their patrols across the Pahang River in the 'loop'. Major D. H. Aubrey-Smith and Company Sergeant-Major Harton did at last bring off one success there. While searching for a camp, whose whereabouts were suspected to be in a fairly closely defined area, they killed one terrorist; with a bit more luck they might have had a bigger bag.

It was at this time, on 17 March 1955, that Lieutenant-Colonel J. L. Brind, soon to be promoted brigadier, handed over command of the Battalion to Lieutenant-Colonel V. S. Baily. Colonel Brind had made sure that the Battalion arrived in Malaya with every intention of making a success of their tour and had seen to it that their initial operations had enabled the Battalion to prove their worth. Later, when responsible for the entire State of Selangor, one of the most difficult tasks in Malaya, he had prevented the Battalion from becoming disheartened by their apparent lack of success. In Pahang he had seen that the launching of the new operations was based on the sound principles which his two years' experience had taught him to be necessary. These principles, when applied by Lieutenant-Colonel Baily, paid their full dividend and enabled him to guide the Battalion to the successful climax of its tour in Malaya.

Higher authority now decided to increase the troops engaged in this operation, and the Northern Rhodesian Regiment was made available. This Regiment was sent to Temerloh to take over from B and C Companies, as it was considered that African troops were better suited to the long jungle operations that were desirable in the Kuala Krau area. B and C Companies were therefore sent to Benta and Raub. A Company was left behind under command of the Rhodesians. D Company remained in the same area as before. The area now to be flooded with troops, as a result of this re-deployment, was bounded to the east by the railway line, to the south by the Bentong-Temerloh road and to the west by the Bentong-Benta road. Inside this vast rectangle of jungle was Thirty-two Platoon. In the past they had been known to move from side to side of the area, calling on the local 'Min Yuen' groups in the Raub area to the west, or in the Kuala Krau area to the east, for supplies as troop activity made it desirable. The new deployment, it was hoped, would prevent this. In addition to these purely tactical reasonings, Raub had a significant strategic importance, for it was in this area that the terrorists still contrived to maintain a tenuous link between their northern and southern organizations. If the 'Min Yuen' groups and their superior organizations in this area could be finally eliminated, it would then be possible to split Malaya into two separate terrorist zones between which communication would be impossible. The tactical and strategic aims behind this new distribution of troops were therefore of considerable importance.

The new deployment made B and C companies responsible for terrorist activities in the west, in the Benta and Raub area. A Company were in the south, along the Semantan River, and the Rhodesians operated in the Kerdau and Kuala Krau areas to the east. Whatever might be thought of moving troops from an area they knew to one in which they would now need up to two months before they could expect to get results, the outcome was startlingly successful for all concerned.

A Company started the ball rolling. Sergeant Bellringer surprised a terrorist just as he was leaving his camp and shot him dead. Corporal D. I. Clements won a Military Medal in a fierce little encounter. The patrol to which he belonged was returning after a week in the jungle, when the leading scout saw bandits in a clearing. He opened fire, as did the bandits with an automatic. The leading men, amongst whom was Corporal Clements, charged to find themselves confronted by a deep swamp of ten-foot-high sword-grass. Corporal Clements, however, found the terrorists' escape route and continued the pursuit. Plunging after them through the swamp, he was fired at by his unseen quarry and wounded in the ear. He fired back and killed one man. The other made good his escape; he surrendered later.

Lieutenant D. Hancock found a Thirty-two Platoon camp that had just been evacuated and, tracking them for three days, narrowly missed being shot in an ambush; he was saved by the quick wits of his Iban tracker who fired first. Thirty-two Platoon fled before his platoon, carrying a newly slaughtered ox, but he lost them when they doubled back to where they had started from. His chase was not, however, in vain, for the Northern Rhodesians took over from where he left off and a few days later attacked another Thirty-two Platoon camp quite near to where Hancock had found their last one. The Rhodesians had a fierce battle in which their white commander was killed, but the terrorists suffered severe losses. These losses gave rise to dissension within the platoon which, coupled with their growing food problems and the increasingly threatening activities of the military, made several of them decide to slip away from their comrades and surrender. A steady trickle from this platoon and from the various 'Min Yuen' groups began to give themselves up. Soon the police station at Mentakab could not house them all; for them it must have been rather like an Old Boys' reunion.

The badly depleted Thirty-two Platoon now decided to turn west and moved over to the Raub area where presumably they hoped for a quieter life and better food. B and C Companies were ready to give them a warm welcome. Directly they arrived near Raub one of the troopers of this platoon surrendered and was at once put to good use. A combined patrol of B and C Companies set out with this man, by name Ah Pee, to find his late camp. It was quickly found in a banana plantation on the jungle edge, but was deserted. The camp fires were still burning, which showed that they had decamped in haste when they realized that Ah Pee had absconded. Lieutenant E. D. Capper, the commander of the pursuit force, started to try to track them down. The bandits were found to have moved in small parties to the jungle edge, where they had mingled their tracks with those of the locals, to try to throw the inevitable pursuers off the trail. This nearly succeeded, but with the aid of a tracker dog, an Iban and Ah Pee himself the spoor was at last picked up. They were now a day behind their quarry. Capper split his force into two: a small and lightly equipped reconnaissance party under himself, and a main party with the rations and heavy equipment.

Meanwhile the terrorists, becoming confident that they had outwitted any pursuers, halted for a day to go hunting. They broke up into two parties and succeeded in killing an iguana and a wild pig. This rich fare made most of them sick and next day they moved on with no particular speed and with no attempt at all at concealing their tracks. Capper followed on, but was delayed a whole morning waiting for additional rations, a delay which was increased by the unfortunate death of one of the carrying party, Private Bessant, so that he could not continue the chase until the afternoon. Luckily the bandits failed to make use of this and only moved a short way themselves. Next day they did not move at all, as they had decided to go hunting again. Capper was still moving in two parties: himself, Corporal Eade, an Iban tracker and an interpreter in a scouting role and a supporting main party of fourteen soldiers under two sergeants. It was at 3.45 on the afternoon of Sunday 26 June 1955 that the Iban indicated that the trail was 'hot'. Packs were dropped on the track for greater freedom of action and the patrol edged forward with all possible precautions. They soon came to a deep gorge in very thick jungle. On the far side steps had been cut in the steep bank. Half-way up the steps a cough was heard and the patrol saw a man lying on a log platform and also the corner of a basha. Capper was now in an awkward predicament: if he went further forward he would be seen; the undergrowth was too thick for a silent encircling manoeuvre, but it would be unwise to go back and give orders to his main party who were now on the far side of the gorge and higher than his group. He decided to attack at once and rely on the common sense of the main body to support him. He and the Iban took careful aim at the prostrate terrorist and fired together. He was shot dead. Another bandit sprang up with a light machine-gun and was shot down by Corporal Eade. This prompt action probably saved the lives of many men in the main party at whom the bandit was aiming. The main party came into action across the gorge and shot another bandit armed with a Sten gun. Another was seen to flee, and a fifth disappeared without being seen at all. The steepness of the slope delayed the attackers, who burst into the camp to find it empty except for the three dead. But for the absence of the terrorist leader on his shooting expedition the bag might have been greater. As it was, the notorious Thirty-two Platoon was now reduced to a total of seven men and had lost their main weapons.

Although Capper had pulled off a notable success his real troubles were only just starting. His first task was to try to follow up the fleeing bandits but although one man's tracks were found, they could not be followed very far. He next turned his attention to the problem of getting the dead terrorists' bodies out of the jungle for definite identification. This was not an easy task for his platoon was now over twenty miles from the nearest road, his whole party was exhausted by the rigours of the chase and their jungle boots were in tatters. There was supposed to be a helicopter landing-zone in the area but after two days' fruitless search for it he had to make his own, using explosives dropped to him by Valetta aircraft. A helicopter from the Royal Navy managed to land, but refused to attempt it a second time, as it was still too small; so that this helicopter only evacuated one man who was seriously ill with an Oriental disease known as leptospirosis. It was now obvious that this platoon could do no more and they were told to come out, which they achieved in one day by making a forced march. Doubtless their desire to get out of the jungle lent speed to their tired feet, for the sense of achievement that success had raised within each man had been sadly dulled by the problems that had beset them since their kill. It is not hard to imagine the feelings of this young National Service officer in this predicament: problems of a seriously sick man, of additional supplies of rations, of new clothing; complications in making a landing-zone, receiving air drops, using explosives; the demand from above to produce the bodies; while his means of communication were a doubtful wireless set and the morse code—a heavy responsibility indeed.

The Battalion's tour in Malaya was rapidly drawing to its close and every effort was made to try to destroy the remnant of this band before it left. On 30 June another gang, the Lanchang 'Min Yuen' group, came to an end. This had been A Company's target on and off, and many hundreds of patrol hours had been fruitlessly spent in search of them. But the fact that this group was eliminated in the end is an interesting example of co-operation between soldiers, police and civilians. The patrolling of the jungle by the soldiers had

made the bandits' life so perilous that they had ceased building camps and had been forced to change their resting-places
daily. The police, under a particularly efficient police lieutenant, had been so thorough in their patrols in the rubber
and so strict in enforcing food control that this terrorist
group were getting desperate. As a result of this the leader
of the gang contacted some villagers and rashly made a rendezvous for the following night in a banana grove. This came
to the ears of the Malay Home Guard leader, who decided to
keep the rendezvous. Under pretext of going fishing he and
some friends paddled their canoes upstream that evening;
later they drifted down with the current. When the bandits
arrived in the banana grove he killed two and severely
wounded the leader, who was captured next day by the police.
Neither police nor military could ever have brought off this
ambush; they would inevitably have been noticed and given
away. The leaderless band wandered impotently around for
some months, out of touch with any other group, as all the
couriers had either been killed or had surrendered, and then
one day gave themselves up. But soldiers in the jungle, police
in the rubber and enforcing food control and civilian co-
operation had completely cleared this area. No single force
on its own could have succeeded.

About this time the same fate overtook the two 'Min Yuen'
branches of Semantan and Belengu. Again all the Security
Forces played their part. Corporal Thatcher, on almost his
last patrol after three years of patrolling, killed two of the
Semantan Branch who were surprised cutting edible palms,
and very soon afterwards the remainder surrendered. In truth,
these successes stemmed from Major Haigh's famous Chinese
New Year's Day attack, just as the destruction of Thirty-two
Platoon stemmed from the Northern Rhodesian attack on
their camp, which in its turn stemmed from Lieutenant
Hancock's chase of that platoon. Once a success had been
achieved, if pressure could be maintained, there would come
a snowball effect.

During all this little mention has been made of D Company. That is not to say that they were idle; far from it. But their operational area eventually proved to be out of touch with the rest of the district and so had little bearing on the main events. In the Menchis area there was a small group of terrorists who survived by their cultivation efforts in the deep jungle. A certain Loh Wah, a hard-core terrorist and expert gardener, was in charge. D Company's efforts to get to grips with Loh Wah were complicated by the presence of aboriginal Sakai who had become enmeshed in the bandit war despite themselves and were being forced to help. These pathetically primitive little people lived deep in the seclusion of the jungle and had no wish whatsoever to be involved, being excessively shy and timid folk who barely contrived to exist in any case. They grew minute crops in clearings, shot game with blow-pipes, dug pig-traps or constructed bamboo and liana spear-traps—very dangerous these to man as well as to beast, as was realized when a Chinese interpreter was speared through both thighs by one such contraption. The Government had tried to help and protect them by grouping those whom they could locate under police surveillance and by providing medical attention. Those soldiers who visited their squalid and unutterably primitive settlements were appalled at the state in which they contrived to survive.

D Company built a large number of helicopter landing-zones near the terrorist cultivations and carried out an endless series of ambushes. It was a tedious game, during which patrol leaders played every trick and tried every subterfuge to entice bandits into their traps. Slowly but surely, but never spectacularly, they whittled down the bandit strength. Lieutenant F. C. Facey and Sergeant O'Reilly both had successful bandit ambushes. Lieutenant C. R. Joynt wounded Loh Wah in another ambush and was lucky enough to have Loh Wah's death of this wound confirmed later by another terrorist who surrendered and led them back to his grave. With Loh Wah dead, there was not much to be feared from this little group, which by then was only about three strong and quite ineffective.

73

D Company were not the only company to make contact with the Sakai. Captain D. R. Goddard and a platoon of C Company carried out one operation, which not only illustrates the problem that these people posed, but is also an excellent example of the detailed planning and preparation that was required to achieve success. The meticulous preparations described here were an essential part of all operations in which chance did not happen to be the over-riding factor. In this case an Auster pilot happened to observe a large cultivation area in the 'loop' of the Pahang River, in which he saw three bashas and some washing on a line. Captain Goddard was flown over the area to see for himself and then a two weeks' pause was allowed in order to allay any suspicion that might have arisen in the minds of the occupants. Meanwhile, air photographs were studied to try to place the camp on the map. Maps and photographs being what they were, this proved impossible, except to indicate that it lay on the east of a long jungle ridge and was on a small stream.

On 28 January 1955 Goddard's platoon were helicoptered into a landing-zone some twenty thousand yards from their objective. Here they hid a large supply of food and the whole platoon moved off carrying six days' supplies to set up a forward base camp. At this camp they split into two: one part under Goddard to operate from this base, while Sergeant Bone returned to the landing-zone to carry out patrolling there on his own account. The advantage of this was that Goddard's own party now had ample food supplies and ought not to need further replenishment from the air, which might well give their presence away. Patrols started the next morning, probing forward with all caution for signs of bandit activity; lest they might inadvertently leave a tell-tale spoor from the pattern of their jungle boots, they wore rubber hockey boots, the normal terrorist foot-gear. That first day one patrol found animal traps, and the next day Goddard followed on from there and located the cultivation area, which was substantiated by comparison of the ground with the air photographs. Although they could not see the camp, they knew where it lay. It was decided to wait until a rainstorm before attacking, the rain, of course, being used to cover the noise of the attackers and deter the bandit sentries from keeping a thorough look-out. Three days without rain followed and on the fourth they were compelled to take an air-drop—a free drop from an Auster, which was less noticeable than one from a Valetta. By the fifth day there was still no rain and Goddard decided to make use of a full moon to try to carry out a night attack or, failing that, one at dawn. They set off a couple of hours before dusk to get into position, leaving a small party in camp including one Iban, who was suffering from dreams of ill-omen, which could not be utterly disregarded, however fanciful. Here the whole plan nearly miscarried. Goddard and another Iban were investigating the track down which they were later to advance, when the Iban suddenly disappeared into a fallen tree. Goddard followed suit hurriedly and four men passed by carrying between them one shotgun and a blow-pipe. They were let by, for night had almost fallen and neither Goddard nor the Iban were in positions from which to open fire.

After dark the patrol crept down the track, using pieces of white paper for a trail, until the brilliant phosphorescence of fallen leaves confused this tactic. They stopped about forty yards from the camp, from which the sound of voices and the smell of a wood fire were quite distinct. Goddard and Corporal McCombe then went forward to spy out the final approach. They failed utterly to find a way through some bushes and returned to wait for the moon to rise higher. A second attempt by these two was equally unsuccessful. Later on, in the middle of the night, there was a burst of activity from the camp: low chattering, the crackle of a fire and the clang of cooking-pots. Goddard eventually decided that there was sufficient noise for the patrol to be able to creep up under cover of it. Hardly had they crept up to about fifteen yards from the bashas before all noise ceased. Goddard withdrew his men—a considerable feat of jungle-craft and self-discipline this. Later, talk again started from the camp, but this time there were only two voices; two had had an early breakfast and gone. At dawn the patrol crept forward to their objective for the last time. Goddard placed his men in position and opened fire on the huts. A man was seen to dart away on the far side of the cultivation area. There was one dead man with a broken shotgun in the riddled bashas. He was a Sakai: one of four unhappy little men enmeshed in the 'emergency', of which he could have known nothing and cared less, but who undoubtedly was helping the terrorists by his cultivation efforts. Despite its sad, almost pathetic outcome, this patrol shows well what care in planning was necessary and what patience and forbearance was needed in execution and, indeed, what a big part was played by chance, even when both planning and execution were, as they were in this case, impeccable.

B and C Companies in the Raub area very nearly completely cleared the area before the Battalion left. Lieutenant R. Hambly accounted for one terrorist who had been wounded the previous day by a police patrol. Lieutenant E. D. Capper killed another in an ambush in a rubber estate. Lieutenant D. C. Wield brought off the last success for the Battalion when, after finding a 'letter box' in a recently used bandit camp, he decided to set an ambush. This letter box was a bottle covered with a tin set in the bole of a tree. He was lucky in only having to wait one day; early on the second morning a terrorist visited the letter box and was killed.

On 9 September 1955 a major change occurred in the policy of the Malayan Government towards the terrorists. An amnesty was declared. The rules for this new game could only have been devised by politicians. Captures and surrenders rather than kills were to be encouraged. If met, bandits were to be challenged and then asked to surrender. Fire was only to be opened if the terrorists showed an aggressive spirit or if the safety of the patrol would be endangered by not doing so. It will be readily appreciated that to a soldier it was not exactly an attractive policy. Luckily, no patrol leader in the Battalion was to be put to this test as, during the short time that remained, there were no contacts with any terrorists. A Malay Regiment patrol had one, however, that illustrates the possibilities. They came on a party of bandits reading the surrender leaflets which they had just scattered. They obediently called out to the bandits to surrender and were immediately fired on, mercifully with no damage. Very few terrorists availed themselves of this amnesty offer and indeed, on the contrary, it seemed that less surrenders of any sort occurred.

On 20 September 1955 the 1st Battalion the Royal Lincolnshire Regiment took over responsibility for the area and the Battalion took train for Singapore. While actually entraining at Kuala Lipis, the news came in that Miew Pak, the leader of the remnants of Thirty-two Platoon, had surrendered. And at Singapore news was received that Phui Wah, the head of the South Pahang Regional Bureau, had also given himself up. During the Battalion's tour in Pahang a terrorist organization of about a hundred had been reduced to some six leaderless men. This operation of nine months had been a classic example of co-operation between the civil administrators, the police and the army.

While in Pahang, the Battalion was visited by many important people. On 8 September 1955 the High Commissioner, Sir Donald McGillivray, visited Bentong and lunched with the officers. The Colonel of the Regiment, Field-Marshal Sir John Harding, managed to visit all the company base camps by helicopter—an unusual achievement for the Chief of the Imperial General Staff. The Director of Infantry, Major-General C. L. Firbank, toured the area and flew into one of D Company's jungle landing-zones. The Director of Operations in Malaya, Sir Geoffrey Bourne, also toured all the company bases to say farewell.

Relaxation from the rigours of the jungle and the boredom of life in company base camps was not only important for reasons of morale, but also on medical grounds. For the first two years in the State of Selangor it was generally possible for men off duty to be occasionally run down to the seaside at Port Dickson, for it was generally considered that sea and sunshine were, on the whole, as good a cure as any medicine for the skin diseases that attacked everyone. Unfortunately most of the coast line of Selangor was mangrove swamp, and Port Dickson was not always within reach. At Kuala Selangor the District Officer lent his motor launch to run men who were off duty to an island off the coast, where they could relax under a lighthouse and bathe in clear water. For the married men there was no problem while the Battalion was in Selangor, for their families were in Kuala Lumpur and, unless on patrol, they could normally spend the night at home.

Pahang was so much more remote and so much more 'jungly' that a different plan had to be made. The married men were normally able to spend a long week-end every four weeks or so in Kuala Lumpur, although a special convoy had to be arranged to get them over the high central ridge pass in safety. For the unmarried men a Battalion leave camp was set up on the golden beaches of Eastern Pahang just north of Kuantan. Here for a week each platoon in turn was able to relax on what must be one of the most perfect beaches in the world with coconut palms running down to the surf. The journey there was a somewhat gruelling undertaking over appalling dirt roads and covering a distance of more than 150 miles, but it was well worth the trouble and was deservedly popular. A Company had a welcome break when they were sent to Kota Bahru in the State of Kelantan, during the first all-Malayan elections, to ensure that no troubles occurred. None did, and the Company spent a happy week bathing in the sea.

One of the major problems confronting all commanders was to decide how much to interfere and how much to remain aloof. The battalion commander had a natural desire to get control of his companies and organize a great operation with himself in command. Very few could resist the temptation of doing this at least once during their period of command. Understandable though this was, it rarely produced anything but frustration. A commanding officer's best policy was generally to allot companies definite areas and give them a free hand to get on with their tasks in their own way. Switching companies at short notice from place to place rarely produced results and sometimes caused accidents. But for a keen commander, this went right against the grain and was directly opposed to all his training and instincts.

The company commander's problem was not dissimilar. If he was a member of one of the combined committees he could not go into the jungle and that was that; but if he had no outside responsibility and was merely controlling his company's activities, he was torn between the desire to go out with his platoons and a wish not to be in the way. For inevitably he was in the way. A platoon had a perfectly capable commander, and an elderly major was probably more of a hindrance than an asset. But he had to go out from time to time to get to know the jungle and then it was better for him to arrange a special headquarters patrol or to go out with a platoon in the absence of its commander. It was rarely wise for him to take the company out in a body. The most remunerative method seemed to be patrols of between ten and twenty men which was, in fact, about an average platoon's strength. Another problem that beset the company commander if he went out himself was the invariable crisis that blew up in his absence and which could not be satisfactorily solved by morse over the wireless. And of course it was barely possible for a company commander with one platoon to control the actions of a second platoon miles away in the jungle, let alone give a considered opinion on the employment of the reserve platoon back in base camp.

These perennial problems beset all commanders and were solved, according to personalities, now this way and now that. On top of these there was the perpetual running fight between company, battalion and brigade headquarters about the moving of any particular company because, for the moment, it appeared to be having no luck where it was.

To sum up the Battalion's tour in Malaya: the initial

period in the North Swamp, operating with unusually good Special Branch information, was a resounding success that started the Battalion off with a fine reputation. The middle period, marked by the operations around Kuala Lumpur, was a frustrating and difficult time, on the whole disappointing in view of the time, energy and thought expended. The final period in Pahang was classically successful and enabled the Battalion to leave Malaya with a record that at that time could not be bettered. Statistically the Battalion killed fifty-four bandits and captured seven, but a truer assessment of its achievement would be the fact that it cleared the North Swamp and South Pahang of terrorists.

On 27 September 1955 the Battalion entrained at various stations down the line for the journey to Singapore by the 'Golden Blow-pipe', to be accommodated temporarily at Nee Soon. The Commander-in-Chief, Sir Charles Loewen, was to have taken the salute at the final parade but, with typical Malayan perversity, the heavens opened to deluge the parade with a cloudburst. The general's address in the gymnasium, where the parade took refuge, was largely inaudible owing to the thunderous drumming of rain on the tin roof. On 28 September the Battalion embarked for England and docked at Liverpool on 27 October 1955, to be met by the Deputy Colonel of the Regiment, Major-General Firbank and the Regimental Band. After surviving a particularly testing inspection by the customs officials and some pilfering by dockers, the Battalion was taken in two trains to Taunton where they were to spend the night.

As the trains approached Somerset, excitement mounted as cheering crowds of friends and relatives were found to be awaiting the Battalion on the platforms from Bristol onwards. Banners, such as 'Set 'em alight Sets', were to be seen on factories as the trains thundered south. At Taunton there was a prodigious assembly to welcome the men of Somerset back to Somerset. The band of the 4th/5th Battalion was largely inaudible amid the clamour of reunions between parents and their sons. Next morning the Battalion paraded

Malaya: The Mortar Platoon in a jungle clearing

A 'C' Company jungle base camp

on the Depot Square for a drum-head service before starting on their triumphal march through the town. For triumphal it was. From the excitement and jubilation of the crowds it might have been thought that the Battalion had returned from the jaws of the nethermost Hell. Great and cheering crowds lined the streets; flags and bunting were up; 'Welcome Home Mike' draped a corner shop—who was Mike? After the march the men were all entertained by the Mayor and Corporation to a civic luncheon before returning to the Depot. Then occurred a fantastic scene. Parents would no longer brook denial of their desire really to meet their sons and by main force invaded the Barrack Square as it has doubtless never been invaded before, and a tumultuously happy scene of jubilation ensued. The real reason for this reception is not hard to find: never before had so many Somerset men been in a Regular battalion of the Regiment, and never before had the County been given a reason and an opportunity to welcome such a battalion as it now was. The Regiment and the County were very close.

That evening the Battalion went on by train to Plymouth, where they were accommodated in Crown Hill Barracks. On 1 November 1955 they all went on leave and did not re-assemble until 1 January 1956 in deep snow. Thus ended a memorable overseas tour with an even more memorable home-coming.

The following were the principal office-holders during the final period in Malaya:

Commanding Officer .	Lieutenant-Colonel V. S. Baily
Second-in-command .	Major C. W. E. Satterthwaite
Adjutant . . .	Captain C. D. C. Frith
Quartermaster . .	Captain T. Meredith, M.B.E.
R.S.M. . . .	R.S.M. K. E. Bartlett
Headquarter Company	Major T. M. Braithwaite, M.C.
	C.S.M. R. G. Gillard
A Company . .	Major K. J. Whitehead, M.C.
	C.S.M. E. A. Giles, M.M.

B Company	. .	Major D. H. Aubrey-Smith, M.B.E. C.S.M. R. Harton (K.S.L.I.)
C Company	. .	Major P. Haigh, M.C. C.S.M. A. J. Longney
D Company	. .	Major T. Lock C.S.M. C. Driver
Support Company	.	Major H. McLean C.S.M. R. Puddy, M.M.

The final list of honours and awards was announced on board ship on the way home: a complete list is set out in Appendix B. Before the Battalion left Pahang and Malaya, a memorial service was held in the cemetery at Kuala Lumpur, where were buried all those who had been killed or had died during the Battalion's tour in Malaya. Small parties from all companies of the Battalion travelled over the high central pass to the capital for this moving ceremony, at which final tributes were paid.

CHAPTER SIX

ENGLAND

The Depot – Sir John Harding Colonel of the Regiment –
Chief Yeoman Warder Cook – Old Colours laid up – Battle
Honours for the Second World War approved – Amalgamation with the Duke of Cornwall's Light Infantry notified –
Majors G. H. Farmer and C. W. Smart – 1st Battalion at
Plymouth – Duties with Territorial camps – Freedom of
Wells – 4th Battalion – Lieutenant-Colonel Roberts hands
over to Lieutenant-Colonel Stewart – 'Z' Reservists – Change
to 4th/5th Battalion – Lieutenant-Colonel Trotman in command – Civil Defence – Changes in National Servicemen's
reserve training commitments – Lieutenant-Colonel Harding
in command – Territorial Golden Jubilee.

In an earlier chapter the re-birth of the Depot from the
remnants of the 13th Primary Training Centre was recorded.
The Depot was commanded by Major A. Hunt, who trans-
ferred from command of the Primary Training Centre to that
of the Depot in April 1948. Major Hunt commanded until
December 1948 when, after a short interregnum under Major
D. J. Boughton, Major P. Lewis assumed command. Major
Lewis commanded until October 1951 when Major J. H. G.
Wells took over.

The new Depot under Major Wells' command was a very
different place to the cloistered establishment of pre-war
days. This was brought about by the fact that the men were
now nearly all Somerset-born, coupled with the fact that they
were mostly National Servicemen. Recruits now arrived in
fortnightly parties for a six weeks' cycle of training at the
end of which they 'passed out' in batches before being posted
to one of the battalions of the Light Infantry Brigade. In
order that parents should take an interest in the well-being

of their sons, they were invited to attend these 'passing out' parades, at which some local dignitary or distinguished soldier took the salute. Later, Parents' Days were instituted in the middle of the training period, which had by then been extended to ten weeks. Both these innovations were popular with parents and recruits and not only gave the parents some idea how their sons were being trained and treated but also enabled them to see for themselves their progress. These were obviously good innovations which brought soldier and civilian closer together; many parents who stormed the Depot square on the return of the 1st Battalion would have been there before to see their sons 'pass out'.

In 1952 occurred the death of His Majesty King George VI, the Colonel-in-Chief of the Regiment. Major Wells took a contingent of twenty men to London to march in the funeral cortège on this sad and solemn occasion.

For the Coronation of Her Majesty Queen Elizabeth II, Major Wells again took a contingent to London to join the other Light Infantry detachments. Some lined the streets and some marched in the procession. Mr. F. Holt, as a representative of the Regimental Association, was given the high honour of a seat in Westminster Abbey for the actual ceremony. On 5 July 1953 Her Majesty reviewed the Ex-Servicemen's associations, in which the Regimental Association took their part.

On 1 November 1952 General Sir John Harding was appointed Chief of the Imperial General Staff and in this capacity the Regiment was frequently honoured by his visits, both abroad and at home. This was the highest position to which any member of the Regiment had risen in the army. It was while holding this high position, on 13 April 1953, that he was appointed Colonel of the Regiment in place of Sir John Swayne. Shortly afterwards, on 21 July 1953, he was promoted to the rank of Field-Marshal. Despite these high honours and arduous duties, the Regiment was to see much of him during these years. When, however, on 29 September 1955 he was appointed Governor and Commander-in-

Chief of Cyprus, then in a state of revolt, it proved impossible for him to continue to carry out his duties as Colonel of the Regiment and he appointed Major-General C. L. Firbank as his Deputy Colonel. Since General Firbank was Director of Infantry, this was a felicitous arrangement, as the Infantry was then in process of being reorganized.

It is perhaps appropriate here to mention another distinguished member of the Regiment, ex-Regimental Sergeant-Major A. H. Cook, D.C.M., M.M., B.E.M., M.S.M., Chief Warder of the Tower of London. Arthur Cook had served in the 1st Battalion in Flanders throughout the First World War from private to company sergeant-major, winning the Distinguished Conduct Medal and Military Medal for gallantry in the field. In 1926 he became Regimental Sergeant-Major of the 2nd Battalion in Khartoum. In 1930 he transferred as Regimental Sergeant-Major to the Depot and finally took his discharge, after twenty-two years' service, in 1932. Later he became a Yeoman Warder at the Tower of London until, in 1943, he became Chief Warder. Before his death in 1957 he had written his First World War Memoirs, which were later published by Major-General Molesworth as *A Soldier's Story*. He had also written a history of the prisoners of the Tower of London, which was printed in a very limited edition after his death and is the only authoritative work on the subject. Other members of the Regiment were also Yeoman Warders when Mr Cook went to the Tower: A. Ellis, D.C.M., Nobby Wilson, M.C., ex-Master Tailor of the 1st Battalion, and Wally Iliffe. Later Yeoman Warders were ex-O.R.Q.M.S. M. Ellis, B.E.M., and ex-Warrant Officer Mike Chapman, M.B.E., both of the 2nd Battalion.

The Depot assumed considerable responsibilities towards the Somerset County Army Cadet Forces, including the cadet forces of several local schools. These were all entitled to wear the Regimental badge. This was an important innovation, which theoretically could have considerable effect on recruiting. They also assisted the Somerset Home Guard until it was disbanded. On 18 October 1952 Major C. C. A. Carfrae assumed command of the Depot, taking over from Major Wells.

In 1955 it was decided to assemble the old Colours of the 1st and 2nd Battalions in the Regimental Museum which, under the care of Lieutenant-Colonel Hunt, now retired and administrative officer to the Depot, had become a proper home and depository of the Regiment's trophies and records. On 9 February 1955 the Queen's and Regimental Colours of the 1st Battalion were removed without ceremony from Wells Cathedral. These Colours had been presented by the Prince Consort in 1846 and had been laid up in 1864. They had been carried in the Crimean War and the Indian Mutiny. The 2nd Battalion Colours were removed from the Parish Church of Saint Mary Magdalene at Taunton at a special ceremony on 9 January 1955. The Colonel of the Regiment, Sir John Harding, received the Colours from the church-wardens and handed them to the Colour party to be marched under escort back to the Depot. There were three Colours: the Regimental Colour presented by the Prince Consort in 1859 and laid up in 1895, which had been carried during the Second Burmese War; and the Queen's and Regimental Colours presented by the Commander-in-Chief, the Duke of Cambridge, in 1895 and laid up in 1927. The Queen's Colours of 1859 had disintegrated.

At this time a Regimental Committee was considering the Battle Honours of the Second World War which were in due course approved by the War Office. The major Battle Honours to be carried on the Colours were: 'Hill 112', 'Mont Pincon', 'Rhineland', 'Rhine', 'North-West Europe 1944–45', 'Cassino 11', 'Cosina Canal Crossing', 'Italy 1944–45', 'North Arakan' and 'Ngakyedauk Pass'.

Other Battle Honours were also approved: 'Odon', 'Caen', 'Noireau Crossing', 'Seine 1944', 'Nederrijn', 'Geilenkirchen', 'Roer', 'Cleve', 'Goch', 'Hochwald', 'Xanten', 'Bremen', 'Trasimene Line', 'Arezzo', 'Florence', 'Capture of Forli', 'Athens', 'Greece 1944–45', 'Buthidaung', 'Burma 1943–44'.

On 12 December 1955 Major T. M. Braithwaite took over

command of the Depot from Major Carfrae. During his tenure of command the decision to amalgamate the Regiment with the Duke of Cornwall's Light Infantry was announced and it was on his shoulders that fell the initial responsibility for the amicable solution of the many problems that arose. The first meetings with the representatives of the Duke of Cornwall's Light Infantry started in the New Year of 1958. It was also in 1955 that Lieutenant-Colonel A. Hunt finally withdrew from his regimental activities and was replaced by Lieutenant-Colonel A. C. M. Urwick as the retired officer of the Regiment at the Depot.

On 19 September 1958 Major C. W. E. Satterthwaite took over command from Major Braithwaite. On him fell the sad honour of being the last Depot Commander of the Somerset Light Infantry; he organized the final smooth amalgamation and closed the barracks, which had been the home of the Regiment for eighty-seven years, since 1873.

However much the passing of the Regiment must be regretted, it is a consolation that there is not an utter void in its place, for assuredly the spirit of the Somerset Light Infantry will live on in the Somerset and Cornwall Light Infantry. That the XIIIth should have been amalgamated with the Duke of Cornwall's Light Infantry, fellow west-countrymen, fellow Light Infantrymen, and a regiment whose 5th Battalion fought alongside the 4th and 7th throughout the last war, is not only a consolation, but also the assurance of a doughty future. The new Regiment is the offspring of two proud and sturdy parents. Most will agree that this reform was necessary, many will think that it was overdue and some will think that it has not gone far enough. The last war proved that the training and reinforcement system could not cope with an infantry organization based on such a small unit as a county regiment, and that some form of grouping in larger units was essential, even if not desirable. The official strengthening of the Light Infantry Brigade and the centralizing of the recruiting and training systems ought to ensure that in the event of another war battalions of the Light Infantry Brigade get Light Infantry men; that must be to the good. Strong though the *esprit de corps* of the new Regiment will be, it will be embraced and fortified by the wider spirit of the Light Infantry.

Before leaving the Depot, mention must be made of two members of the Regiment of outstanding merit whose military careers ended there: Majors George Farmer and Ben Smart, each of whom finished his career as Quartermaster at Taunton. To many generations of officers and men they represented the Somerset soldier at his best. Major Smart joined the Regiment as a recruit in 1923 and retired thirty-six years later in 1959 as a Major Quartermaster decorated with the M.B.E. Twenty-seven of those years were spent with the 1st Battalion, with which he served in Belfast, Egypt, China, India, Burma, Germany and Malaya. He became a member of the sergeants' mess in 1931 and on the outbreak of the Second World War was a platoon sergeant-major. By 1940 he was Regimental Quartermaster-Sergeant and in 1942 became the Regimental Sergeant-Major of the 1st Battalion. In June 1943 he was commissioned as Quartermaster and was then successively with the 1st Battalion, the Depot, the 4th Battalion, the 1st again and finally at the Depot; a career of unswerving service and loyalty to his Regiment.

Major Farmer served his County Regiment for thirty-eight years. His first period of service was as a Territorial when he joined the 5th Battalion in 1913. On the outbreak of the First World War, this battalion was embodied, and Farmer served with it in India, Egypt and Palestine, rising to the rank of sergeant. In 1919 he enlisted in the Regular Army and joined the 2nd Battalion, with which he served in Palestine, Egypt, India and the Sudan. By 1920 he was again a member of the sergeants' mess and in 1927 was a company sergeant-major. In 1935 he became Regimental Sergeant-Major of the 1st Battalion in Poona, following the famous Paddy O'Hare. At Multan in 1941 he was given a quartermaster's commission and continued to serve with the

1st Battalion until in 1943 he returned to England to become quartermaster of a succession of training establishments connected with the Regiment. These eventually merged into the 2nd and then into the amalgamated 1st Battalion at Bordon. In 1949, having become a Member of the Order of the British Empire, he went to the Depot where he served until his retirement in 1951. A more typical and loyal representative of the County and the Regiment it would be hard to find. These two men are prime examples of the quartermasters' fraternity, on whose shoulders lie such heavy burdens, and whom commanding officers implicitly expect to achieve the impossible.

The 1st Battalion re-assembled at Crown Hill Barracks at Plymouth soon after 1 January 1956. They were one of the few Regular army battalions in England and, as such, might be expected to be required to reach a high standard of training in modern European warfare; this was particularly important, as for three years in Malaya they had never operated as companies, let alone as a battalion. Almost at once, however, although earmarked for emergency overseas roles at any time, they were warned that they would be responsible for assisting Territorial and Cadet Force camps during the summer. As companies to run these camps would have to be in position by 1 May, this only left the two wintry months of February and March for training. At the time this was viewed with grave misgivings within the Battalion and, in view of events later that year, these misgivings were to be proved only too well-founded. It is, in fact, quite unacceptable for Regular army units to be so misused for so long a part of the year. February and March were therefore spent in training on Dartmoor despite the elements, which were not propitious. Although full benefit could not be expected from training in these conditions, some progress was made.

In early May 1956 the three active rifle companies were sent off to prepare their camps in Cornwall. The fourth rifle company, in Plymouth, had already been turned into a training company. This left Lieutenant-Colonel Baily at Plymouth with only two active companies, Support and Headquarter Companies, both in need of all the training with their new weapons and equipment that they could get. As the rifle companies were not expected to be freed from their camp responsibilities until late September, it did not look like being a particularly profitable year. One happy event in this period was the arrival of the 4th/5th Battalion at Plasterdown Camp, run by D Company, which enabled the Regulars and Territorials to see a lot of one another and exchange hospitality.

On 25 April the Regiment was honoured with the Freedom of the City of Wells. Both the 1st and 4th/5th Battalions, as well as the Depot, sent large detachments and the bands and bugles of both battalions were on parade. The 1st Battalion spent one night en route at Taunton, and the whole parade assembled after lunch in the City of Wells to march to the Cathedral where, before a large and distinguished congregation, the Bishop of Bath and Wells officiated at the service. After the service the parade marched to the Market Square to form a.hollow square for the presentation of the Freedom. Major-General C. L. Firbank, the Deputy Colonel of the Regiment, acting for Field-Marshal Sir John Harding who was unable to leave Cyprus, received the Freedom from the Mayor. After the ceremony the parade marched through the streets of the City with both bands playing and carrying the Colours of the 1st and 4th Battalions.

The whole parade was then entertained at a civic tea in the Bishop's Barn. This was followed by an inspired sounding of Retreat on the Cathedral Green, where the 1st Battalion Band and Bugles surpassed themselves in that incomparable setting. The officers of the Regiment then entertained the City and other important guests at a cocktail party. By now unofficial celebrations had got under way and the Cathedral City showered hospitality on the soldiers. Dancing in the Bishop's Barn with free beer and cider went on all through the evening, and beer flowed freely from many a public house until a hilarious night was brought to a close. The enthusiasm and friendliness of the good citizens of Wells could not have been exceeded nor, indeed, the liberality with which good cheer was dispensed. As at Taunton in 1955, the Regiment and County were very close.

On 31 May the Battalion found the military Royal Guard of Honour on the occasion of the Queen's Birthday parade on Plymouth Hoe with the other two services.[1] But storm-clouds were gathering and neither ceremonial occasions nor Cadet Force camps were to be of much importance for some time. On 1 August 1956 a message was received warning the Battalion that it was at seven days' notice to go overseas.

The re-forming of the 4th Battalion under Lieutenant-Colonel W. Q. Roberts was mentioned in Chapter two, as were some of their earlier public appearances. Colonel Roberts, who had joined the Territorials in 1933 and commanded both the 5th Wiltshires and the 4th Dorsets in the 43rd Division during the Second World War, had to re-form his battalion from scratch. In this he was supported by many who had given staunch service to the Regiment in the Second World War. As the newly re-formed battalion was recruiting from the whole of Somerset, amongst those who volunteered from the earliest days were Captains C. J. Stewart, E. A. Trotman, L. D. Wardle, J. C. Perks and J. M. F. Hutchinson, who had all served with the 4th Battalion; from former members of the 5th Battalion came Majors C. M. B. Kite, G. D. Bond, T. H. Harding, and Lieutenants T. U. Taylor, P. J. and T. A. B. Mahoney and R. W. Viveash. In addition, Bugle-Major Wiltshire, Bandmaster Golledge, Company Sergeant-Majors Williams and Hucker, Sergeants Burnell and Seager, Privates Hunt, Vaughan, Topper Smith, Saunders, Langford and R. Wiltshire volunteered in their

[1] The Battalion was to find the military Royal Guard of Honour again in 1957, on its return from Cyprus and before going to Warminster. On this second occasion they added notably to the colour of an inter-service ceremony by parading for the first time in the new Number One Dress of green peaked caps, green jackets, blue trousers and white accoutrements.

respective ranks, thus helping to build a solid basis to the Battalion. All these were dedicated men. Initial Regular support was provided by Captain G. W. Stead as Adjutant, Lieutenant C. F. Male as Quartermaster and Regimental Sergeant-Major W. L. C. Tilley.

The first post-war camp was at Weymouth in July 1948, where the Battalion concentrated on the more elementary aspects of soldiering. Annual camp in July 1949 was at Mytchett, where training was more advanced; with the 1st Battalion near by at Bordon the newly re-formed Territorials were able to meet their Regular counterparts with mutual profit. 1949 saw the introduction of a Regular training major in addition to the other Regular staff, and Major V. S. Baily was the first to hold this appointment as second-in-command. This appointment was intended to help the Territorial commanding officer in the planning and execution of training and lasted until 1959 when, for reasons of manpower economy, it was suppressed and these duties fell on the Regular adjutant, as before the war.

In June 1950 the 4th Battalion went to annual camp at the School of Infantry at Warminster, then commanded by Brigadier C. L. Firbank, and were able to profit from the various demonstrations and exercises available. The fact that their brigade, 130th Infantry Brigade, was then commanded by Brigadier J. R. I. Platt, who had recently been a senior member of the School of Infantry Staff, probably ensured that they received maximum help. In July 1950 Winston Churchill, then Prime Minister, was given the Freedom of the City of Bath. The 4th Battalion provided the Guard of Honour. The last time Mr Churchill had seen the Regiment was when, in the company of Field Marshal Smuts and Mr Mackenzie King, he had toured the army's assembly areas just before they embarked for Normandy in 1944. In March they also provided a Guard of Honour for Princess Elizabeth at Newton Park, when she too visited Bath.

In June 1951 Brigadier Platt took the whole of 130th Infantry Brigade to camp at Castle Martin in Pembrokeshire to take part in brigade operations and co-operate with tanks.

In 1952, after five years in command, Lieutenant-Colonel W. Q. Roberts handed over to Lieutenant-Colonel C. J. Stewart. Colonel Roberts was, however, not lost to the army, for he was promoted colonel and appointed Deputy-Commander of the brigade. Colonel Stewart, with Regular support from Major T. D. Luckock and Captain T. M. Braithwaite, was confronted with a novel and testing problem for the 1952 camp at Windmill Hill on Salisbury Plain, for it had been decided to call up for part-time service some 750 men from the 'Z' Reserves, and these men were to attend fifteen days' training with the Battalion. This was a result of a War Office decision to test the system of calling-up the general army reserve and of giving these men some modern training; the men involved were of that vast category of soldiers who, having seen service during the Second World War, were all technically a reserve to their county regiments. As the 4th Battalion then consisted of some 240 Territorial volunteers and some 190 National Servicemen still under a reserve commitment to attend annual camp, the strain on the Battalion can be imagined. These Reservists arrived at camp straight from civilian life, to be immediately issued with a complete set of clothing and equipment, to be given their tasks and allotted to their sub-units, and then to take part in battalion and brigade exercises. Before returning to civilian life, all their military impedimenta had to be handed in again. Suffice it to say that it was achieved. In October, the Band and Bugles joined a Guard of Honour from the Depot for the Duke of Edinburgh, when he visited Taunton.

Annual camp in June 1953, at the Practical Training Area at Stanford in Norfolk, was a normal camp with only the Territorial volunteers and National Servicemen carrying out their reserve commitment. It was a profitable period at this exceptionally fine training area.

The year 1954 saw the title of the Battalion changed to the 4th/5th Battalion. Before the Second World War there had been the 4th Battalion based on Bath and the north and east of the County, and the 5th Battalion, based on Taunton and the south and west. During the First World War both battalions had seen active service in the Near East. Shortly before the Second World War the Territorial Army had been doubled by Leslie Hore-Belisha, the Secretary of State for War, and the 6th and 7th Battalions had been formed from the 4th and 5th respectively. Later, other battalions had been formed from these, but in fact only the 4th and 7th had seen action, representing both the original Territorial battalions. It was thus only just that both numbers should be incorporated in the one surviving Territorial battalion permitted to the Regiment. But there were two other reasons for the change of title: one was the lack of recruits from the old 5th Battalion area: the other was property, silver and funds belonging to the 5th. By changing the name, the 4th/5th Battalion could hope to improve their recruiting throughout the County and could legally acquire the funds and property that were rightly theirs.

In June 1954 annual camp was held at Fort Tregantle in Cornwall. Despite appallingly bad weather, which seriously interfered with training on Dartmoor, the Battalion did take part in a long brigade exercise. Owing to the presence of large numbers of National Servicemen they went to camp some 800 strong. The number of National Servicemen attending camp continued to increase each year, so that at Tilshead, in September 1955, the Battalion was over 1,100 strong. As that year it had been decided to concentrate the whole 43rd Wessex Division for divisional manœuvres, the numbers of men deployed were considerable. Lieutenant-Colonel E. A. Trotman, who had taken over command from Lieutenant-Colonel Stewart, now promoted colonel and appointed Deputy Brigade commander, had thus a full-strength battalion to manœuvre on what turned out to be a great thermonuclear exercise in the most up-to-date manner. Later that year, during the celebrations commemorating the anniversary of the granting of a charter to Glastonbury, the Battalion found a Guard of Honour for Sir John Harding.

There were two major changes in the Territorial Army in 1956. The first was the emphasis now placed by the Government on Civil Defence, which meant that all but two territorial divisions would be trained mainly for this role. Of the two divisions that were still to be part of an expeditionary force, the 43rd Division was chosen as one—a high honour; this, however, did not prevent them from paying considerable attention to Civil Defence in all future training, and some special exercises were run to this effect. The second change was a reduction in the reserve commitment of the National Servicemen from three annual camps to one. Of the 1,000 men on the Battalion's strength, some 800 were National Servicemen, whether volunteers or non-volunteers. The non-volunteers had therefore already completed their commitment. The volunteers were given the option of remaining or resigning; about ninety decided to continue to volunteer, the rest left. The Battalion was then found to consist of about 120 original Territorials, another ninety from the National Service volunteer element and another ninety National Servicemen doing their one and only annual camp: a total strength of about three hundred men.

Despite the serious reduction in strength, the change was not at all unwelcome to the Territorials, who were firm believers in the volunteer spirit and had never much liked having to cater for a forced element. In addition they had considered that the fact that National Servicemen had to go to camp by law had deterred many men from becoming volunteers. This change completely altered the aspect and aim of the Battalion; from now on they would have to concentrate on recruiting, on recruiting only the best and on training and developing leaders. To achieve this, Colonel Trotman organized a series of recruiting and training weekends at widely dispersed points all over the county. Accordingly annual camp in 1956 at Plasterdown, near Plymouth, was attended by only 300 men, most of whom were volunteers. This camp, in huts as opposed to tents, was popular and, with the 1st Battalion at Plymouth, a good deal of reciprocal entertainment was possible between Regulars and Territorials.

This year Bandmaster Golledge, who had re-formed the Battalion band when the Battalion was reconstituted, retired after forty-two years' service. Also this year Colonel G. W. R. Bishop gave up his appointment as Honorary Colonel and was replaced by Major-General Firbank.

In 1957 the 4th/5th Battalion went to annual camp in May at Windmill Hill near Tidworth. They had present twenty officers and 135 men, but by January 1958 this figure had been increased to 213. Later in 1957 they took part in a full-scale Civil Defence exercise in the City of Bath in conjunction with rescue teams and fire brigades from all over the County. This was a typical week-end camp which has been such a practical feature of Territorial training since the war, and which illustrates the way in which Territorials spend that period when others are engaged in personal pleasures.

In May 1958 Lieutenant-Colonel Trotman was promoted colonel and handed over command to Lieutenant-Colonel T. H. Harding, who continued to command during the period when the Regular part of the Regiment was being amalgamated with the Duke of Cornwall's Light Infantry. After a period of some doubt as to their future name and employment, it was found that the 4th/5th Battalion were to be the only portion of the Regiment to continue to use the old designation of 'Somerset Light Infantry (Prince Albert's)'.

1958 was the year of the Territorial Army Golden Jubilee. A representative detachment went to London for the Review in Hyde Park. Later, in July, parades were held in honour of this occasion at Wells, Taunton and Yeovil. Also in July a detachment took part in the Bath Tattoo. Annual camp that year was at Plasterdown in June. In 1959 the Battalion attended annual camp in April at Chickerell near Weymouth. where they went to sea in Royal Naval frigates and submarines, practised amphibious warfare at Poole and visited the Royal Armoured Corps school at Bovington.

En route for Malta 1956. Lance-Corporal Brayne

Recruiting was considered high priority by Colonel Harding who continued to run recruiting week-ends all over the County. On a typical week-end, apart from training, Retreat was sounded by the band and bugles on the Saturday evening and there was a church parade on the Sunday. Although results were not spectacular, by the autumn of 1959 the Battalion was three hundred strong. And so, on this hopeful note for the future, this period in the history of the Regiment and of the Territorials comes to an end. From now on it was to be the Territorials alone who bore the name 'Somerset Light Infantry (Prince Albert's)', and, as the sole remaining unit, dropped from their title the numerals '4th' and '5th'.

CHAPTER SEVEN

MALTA AND CYPRUS 1956

Mobilization – Reservists – By air to Malta – Training in
Malta – The 'Mutinies' – By aircraft-carrier to Cyprus –
Internal security duties in Cyprus – Return to England.

ON 2 August 1956, as a result of mobilization orders, the
rifle companies of the 1st Battalion came in from their
Territorial camps and the Battalion prepared for war. New
equipment, new weapons, vehicles and stores were collected.
Baggage was packed: sea freight to go independently, and air
kit to go with the men. Everyone was inoculated. It was a
hectic change over from a leisurely peace to sudden war. The
Government had decided to take military action against the
Egyptians and to re-occupy the Suez Canal. The 1st Battalion
was part of the large all-services expedition mobilized for
this purpose.

On 7th August Lieutenant-Colonel Baily and Captain
Meredith, the Quartermaster, with a small advance-party,
reported in all haste to Farnborough to fly ahead; they were
still there, mad with frustration, a week later. The new
motor transport and sea baggage was sent to Barry Docks
in Wales for loading on to a transport vessel. Meanwhile
some two hundred Reservists began to arrive: they were
mostly from the King's Own Yorkshire Light Infantry and
the King's Shropshire Light Infantry and many had already
seen service in Korea or in Kenya. The Battalion was now
thirty-three per cent Reservist. On top of this activity came
a constant stream of urgent and secret messages variously
changing the method, time and place of the Battalion's departure. The Second-in-Command, Major Carfrae, made
new loading tables daily. On 13 August the commanding
officer and quartermaster flew to Malta and next day Major

Ogilvie took another advance-party to join him. Finally the Battalion emplaned on 16 August at Hurn and Black-bushe airports to be flown smoothly and impeccably by British Overseas Airways' Britannias to Malta. Meanwhile, in order to ensure that nothing should remain as it had been, the Battalion was transferred from the 2nd to the 3rd Infantry Brigade.

At Malta the Battalion was housed in a summer camp at Ghadira on a neck of land with the Mediterranean on both sides. This was fortunate for, with the summer heat, the dust and the lack of fresh water, the sea became a necessity to keep clean and cool. Immediately the Battalion set about completing section, platoon, company and battalion training within one month, for they might be launched into action at any moment. Daily they strove to weld themselves into an efficient fighting machine by marching and manœuvring over the bare and dusty hills. It was a strenuous time and all ranks entered into the spirit of the endeavour: to become a serviceable battalion as fast as possible. After the day's labour, all who could relaxed on the sandy beaches of Mellieha Bay.

By November, Malta had become all too small for further training and, with the endless stream of rumours and conjecture and the unhealthy agitation in the popular press, the Battalion needed a change. Companies made independent trips to the Island of Gozo either by the ferry or by co-operating with the Royal Navy. Many men went to sea in the vessels of the First Destroyer Flotilla, H.M.S. *Chieftain*, H.M.S. *Chevron* and H.M.S. *Chaplet* as also in the cruiser H.M.S. *Jamaica*. This was wise, for it was at this time that troubles broke out elsewhere when groups of Reservists mutinied in several regiments.

With the nation split almost evenly as to the wisdom of the venture, it was not unnatural that there were men who thought, with reason, that the whole expedition was lunatic; there were others who no doubt resented being recalled to the Colours; others again were just fed up doing nothing definite; some were perhaps trouble-makers. But without a shadow of doubt the initial troubles were started by the press, exaggerated by the press, and then fanned by the press until there were genuine troubles for the press to report. Whatever anyone might have personally thought of the enterprise, this attitude was surely quite inexcusable. The Regiment has much for which to thank all ranks of the 1st Battalion in that during this worrying time there was no breath of trouble which might tarnish its name. Not even the most seditious reporter could find one word or incident to magnify, fan or distort.

Rumours were rife as to the Battalion's eventual destination. The commanding officer and quartermaster actually went twice to Libya, to make preliminary arrangements for relieving units of the armoured division stationed there. One plan was that the Battalion should take over internal security duties in certain parts of Tripoli from the 3rd Royal Horse Artillery; another was that they should replace the Bays at Sabratha and in another part of Tripoli after staging at a place called Tarhuna in the desert. This second plan carried with it the additional responsibility for some forty polo ponies belonging to the cavalrymen. And of course there was always the chance of going to Suez in a follow-up role. No plans were made for a move to Cyprus. So from the planning point of view this stay in Malta was busy.

But at last all rumours were stilled, when the Battalion embarked in H.M.S. *Ocean* on 11 November for Cyprus. This was a model move, with the whole Battalion accommodated in one great hangar and all the transport lashed to the flight-deck. The rare opportunity of having a whole battalion under one roof was not wasted on Regimental Sergeant-Major Bartlett, and so efficiently and smartly did he run this hangar that an admiral who happened to be aboard, was induced to visit it personally, and was so impressed by what he saw that he wrote to the Colonel of the Regiment in praise.

Arriving on 13 November in an already overcrowded Cyprus, the Battalion was lodged in Kermia camp near

Nicosia, the capital of the island: a dusty camp in dry weather and, come wet, a quagmire. At once they were committed to a host of static guard duties: the central prison, a detention camp, the military hospital and three police stations. But in common with the rest of the Security Forces in Cyprus their main task was the defeat of *Eoka*, the Greek-Cypriot terrorist organization commanded by 'Colonel Grivas'. To this end they organized cordon and search operations and carried out ambushes and snap-checks. From time to time they provided the stand-by force for emergencies in Nicosia. Their area of operations was in the villages around the capital and in Nicosia itself, where the Greek-Cypriot quarter of the old, walled town was a happy hunting-ground for *Eoka* murderers and saboteurs.

Although the active members of *Eoka* were small in actual numbers, they had the sympathy and often the active support of almost the entire Greek-Cypriot population. Every Greek-Cypriot male between the ages of fourteen and twenty-seven was suspect, schoolgirls and even matrons were active supporters, and the whole situation was bedevilled by the conspiracy of silence which, either from sympathy or fear of reprisals, effectively prevented any Greek-Cypriot from overtly aiding the Security Forces. This situation had been brought about by a sustained and ruthless campaign of intimidation of the Greek-Cypriot population by the terrorists. Those with recent experience of Malaya found that the situation was in many ways very different. To them it seemed that the restrictions imposed on the Cypriots were far lighter, and that the population was allowed much greater freedom to move about the island. In fact the situation in Cyprus was more akin to that difficult time when the Battalion was operating in the thickly populated suburbs of Kuala Lumpur, than to the situation in remote and barely inhabited Pahang, where any restrictions could not only be imposed but enforced. The fact that the Malayan Chinese were such willing informers, and that the Greek-Cypriot was so stubbornly silent, accentuated the difference and, of course, the problem for both policeman and soldier.

The Battalion's recent experience of fighting terrorism in Malaya stood it in good stead. They were launched on operations almost as soon as they arrived and with a much shorter period of training than was normally allowed a newly arrived battalion. Once again they found the well-known system of War by Committee, which similar operations in Malaya and Kenya had shown to be indispensable for success. Daily the commanding officer attended 'Morning Prayers' to discuss with the District Commissioner, the police and the intelligence officers what was happening and to be given orders by the brigadier. He then had to hurry back to the Battalion to issue orders for the following day. Speed was essential, as to-morrow's operations generally started to-day. This was necessary if surprise was to be achieved, and many a time companies set out soon after midnight for a night-approach march through the olive orchards, up a dry riverbed or over the fields, so as to be in position around a suspect village before first light. At dawn the villagers would find themselves encircled: the women confined to their homes and all able-bodied men summoned to a prisoner cage for interrogation by Special Branch. Meanwhile the soldiers started a methodical search of every house, backyard and garden. This search was a painstaking business; it meant looking for false floors, dummy ceilings, hidden weapons, explosives or clandestine literature. However distressing it may have been for both searcher and searched, it was abundantly necessary. It was rare for the men to be back in camp before the late afternoon. Perhaps a few documents had been confiscated, an empty pipe-bomb had been found and a few suspects handed over to Special Branch for further interrogation. Again, this was not unlike the thousands of hours of fruitless 'jungle-bashing' which, however futile they seemed at the time, were nevertheless equally necessary.

Eoka made use of strange hiding-places for their weapons and supplies. Cemeteries had been used in the past, and the men found it ghoulish work searching them. Churches were also favourite hiding-places and when these had to be searched a padre was part of the investigating force, lest allegations of sacrilege should later be made. When villages were searched, women of the W.R.A.C. were used to deal with the female inhabitants. Despite all these searches, stratagems and ambuscades, the Battalion did not succeed in bringing off any major arrest. On the other hand they suffered no casualties from *Eoka* activity. The nearest thing to an accident was the ambushing of Lieutenant D. Hancock, who was returning to camp at dusk with two jeeps, when a couple of mines were electrically exploded under them, happily with no serious damage. On another occasion, Private Overd, Major Aubrey-Smith's driver, was sharp enough to detect some home-made bombs secreted in a cemetery wall, which probably prevented a nasty accident later. To guard against surprise attacks, there were very strict rules in force regulating the movements of men and vehicles, both on and off duty: men had to go about in fours, two in front and two behind; everyone was always armed; trucks had to have two armed men in the rear, and by night had to move in pairs. This was admirably sensible. But it is not improbable that the hard core of men with previous experience of terrorism helped to ensure, while the Battalion was in Cyprus, that only one man was slightly wounded in a firearm accident, and that their experienced wariness produced throughout the Battalion a state of vigilance which effectively deterred *Eoka* from attempting to molest them.

Sir John Harding was Governor and Commander-in-Chief of the Island at this time and visited the Battalion on several occasions. He and Lady Harding were able to entertain many officers and all the Warrant officers and sergeants at Government House, which was much appreciated in contrast to the primitive conditions in Kermia camp.

The Reservists, who had by then proved themselves a staunch band of stalwarts amongst so many youthful National Servicemen—rather different to the behaviour of Reservists in some other regiments—returned to England at the end of the year, arriving home on 31 December. They were sadly missed by the Battalion, not only on account of their experience, but also on the score of numbers. From then on, guard duties weighed heavily on the gravely attenuated Battalion. Their numbers were well below the economic strength for a battalion engaged in internal security duties, there was no prospect of adequate reinforcements coming out and before long it was decided to send them back to England. They embarked at Limassol, on the *Empire Ken*, for a quiet passage home to Southampton, where they arrived on 22 January 1957. From there they went on leave, to reassemble in due course at their previous barracks at Crown Hill, Plymouth.

CHAPTER EIGHT

SUEZ 1956

The Anti-Tank Platoon – 42nd Royal Marine Commando –
Landing at Port Said – List of office-holders.

WHILE the 1st Battalion, mobilized against the Egyptians, was marooned in Malta or combating *Eoka*, the Anti-Tank Platoon, under Captain D. T. L. Beath, was embarked on an exploit of its own. On arrival at Malta, they were immediately detached from the Battalion and were sent off with the two other anti-tank platoons of the brigade to an artillery practice camp to be trained in the use of seventeen-pounder anti-tank guns. On return from Malaya they had been issued with the latest anti-tank weapons and had learnt how to handle them. Now, however, these had been taken away and they were to be trained in the use of the guns which had been in service at the end of the Second World War and which none of them had ever seen before.

For the next month, accordingly, they were at the mercy of a gunnery instructor and had soon fired so many rounds out to sea from their weapons that they succeeded in wearing them out. They were then adjudged competent, were issued with six brand-new guns and their Stuart tracked towers and were attached to 42nd Royal Marine Commando, who had no anti-tank weapons of their own. The hectic gunnery training was exchanged for equally hectic marine exercises with countless assault-landing practices on the Maltese beaches on which, by behaving as true Light Infantrymen, they more than held their own. Very soon they had become an integral part of their marine commando.

On 31 October the platoon embarked in the Tank Landing Craft *Counterguard* for yet another exercise. After two days at sea, however, it became apparent that this was to be more than an exercise and, on the fourth day out, they were

Suez 1956

officially briefed on their role in the Port Said assault-landing. All were up at 4 a.m. on 6 November to find that they were now part of an allied armada, the French navy having joined them during the night, and that they were steaming into an unnaturally red dawn which soon resolved itself into burning fires along the low coast, over which hung a pall of smoke and in and out of which wheeled aircraft of the Fleet Air Arm. The assault troops, including the platoon gun detachment commanders, went ashore in assault craft followed by Centurion tanks wading through the sea. The platoon landed some fifteen minutes later in the fishing harbour of Port Said and roared ashore ready for instant action. They soon joined up with the gun commanders and their respective commando units. Armed Egyptians, some in uniform but most in plain clothes, scurried and scattered in all directions. The Royal Marines were busy clearing a tall block of buildings, from which the Egyptians were firing with bazookas, automatics and grenades, and the anti-tank detachments had sporadically to make use of their personal weapons against groups of attackers. No Russian tanks, with which the Egyptians were reported to be armed, presented themselves as targets, but one gun team cleared a garage strong-point of its occupants, who had been harrying the marines, with one well-aimed and spectacular round.

By dusk the battle for the town was over; to the members of the Anti-Tank Platoon it had seemed somehow unreal, so swiftly had come the anti-climax after the initial excitement, the danger and the confusion of the assault. But this short-fought battle had none the less exacted its price. During the morning a Fleet Air Arm pilot in his low-flying aircraft had regrettably mistaken his target and had attacked a gun detachment; Corporal George Crawford, a Reservist, who had served with the Special Air Service Regiment and the Regiment in Malaya, was killed and Private Penny was seriously wounded.

Soon the Platoon was able to park their guns, move off the beaches and take up their quarters in the comfort of a nearby block of flats. They now became riflemen and took their part in helping to restore and maintain law and order in the captured town. Their duties mainly involved collecting heaps of assorted foreign weapons lying scattered about the streets, and in preventing mobs of Egyptians looting and pillaging. In due course the United Nations force arrived and the Platoon embarked for Cyprus, where they at once rejoined the Battalion. They were some of the very few of the vast force mobilized in England and Germany actually to take part in the object of the whole operation.

Thus ended one of the most curious military adventures ever to be undertaken by the British Army: certainly the most curious in which it has been the fortune of the Regiment to take part. One would have to go back to some of the odder military ventures in the early stages of the Napoleonic Wars to find anything comparable.

The principal office-holders during the Suez crisis were as follows:

Commanding Officer .	Lieutenant-Colonel V. S. Baily
Second-in-command .	Major C. C. A. Carfrae, M.C.
Adjutant . . .	Captain R. B. Robertson
Quartermaster . .	Captain T. Meredith, M.B.E.
R.S.M. . .	R.S.M. K. E. Bartlett
A Company . .	Major E. J. Kingston
	C.S.M. R. Puddy, M.M.
B Company . .	Major D. H. Aubrey-Smith, M.B.E.
	C.S.M. R. G. Gillard
C Company . .	Major G. F. Duckworth
	C.S.M. A. J. Longney
D Company . .	Major M. C. Watts
	C.S.M. S. Bolton
Headquarter Company	Major J. M. Ryall
	C.S.M. A. Lambird
Support Company .	Major J. J. Ogilvie, M.B.E.
	C.S.M. A. Morris
Bandmaster . .	Bandmaster N. F. Hirst (with the band in England)

CHAPTER NINE

ENGLAND AND AMALGAMATION 1957–60

1st Battalion at Warminster – Trials and Demonstrations –
Lieutenant-Colonel W. R. Lawson in command – Amalga-
mation and retirement stresses – New arrangements for
Depots and training establishments – Farewell parade.

SHORTLY after returning from Cyprus, the 1st Battalion were
informed that they had been selected for the honourable,
and at the same time highly responsible, distinction of being
the next Demonstration Battalion at the School of Infantry
at Warminster. Although they were not due to take over
officially until early in 1958, it soon became apparent that
quite a lot of men would be required before then to help
out The Royal Inniskilling Fusiliers, who were at the
moment the Demonstration Battalion. In fact, they found
some men for the Annual Demonstration in 1957. The period
of preparation was by no means an easy one for after Suez
the Battalion had dwindled to between two and three hundred men. This deficiency was eventually made good but,
as the vast majority of the new men did not arrive before
September, it was no easy task to train these new arrivals
sufficiently for them to be able to play their parts in demonstration squads in November.

Although the role of Demonstration Battalion was an
honour, it was essentially a negative one from the point of
view of the senior officers and, in particular, from the commanding officer's point of view. The School was responsible
for nearly everything and little was left to the initiative of
the Battalion; all they had to do was to provide trained men
in certain numbers at certain times with certain equipment
at certain places. On the other hand, there was the very real
interest in being at the centre of Infantry thought and

doctrine and in being able to use the latest arms and equipment in unlimited quantities. In addition, from the married man's point of view it was most attractive, as he knew for certain that he would be in one place for two whole years, a very rare event in the post-war infantry world. So, although the job might prove at times frustrating, it had much to commend it. This is not to imply that the School ran the Battalion: far from it. Company and platoon commanders were in command and were naturally the channel through which orders were passed. In many cases improvements to demonstrations were brought about by suggestions made by members of the Battalion.

Before going to Warminster they were involved in a series of trials of new equipment and clothing which they tested on the hills of Dartmoor. One item of equipment, a man-handled trolley, was eventually demonstrated before the assembled generals at the Chief of the Imperial General Staff's annual conference at Camberley. This was a success.

The Battalion lived at Knook Camp near Warminster. The camp was composed of rather inadequate huts and was inconveniently far from the School. Demonstration detachments had also to be provided at three other army schools: a platoon at Eaton Hall Officer Cadet School, later to move to Mons Officer Cadet School; a detachment at the Small Arms Wing at Hythe; and a Support Company detachment at the Heavy Weapons Wing of the School of Infantry at Netheravon. By January 1958 the whole Battalion had moved to the School of Infantry and had begun to learn their new duties. The soldiers soon learnt enough to be able to advise their student officer commanders on exercises as to the best solutions to the problems. But of course exercises were constantly changing, however slightly, as were the men, so that full rehearsals were always needed. The School staff, however, soon learnt with some pleasure that Light Infantry men needed fewer rehearsals than had previous regiments and they were surprised at the speed with which the Battalion reacted to their requests. As Demonstration Battalion

arewell Parade, Knook Camp, 1959: The 1st Battalion marching past the
Colonel of the Regiment

The Colours of the 1st and 2nd Battalions

they were responsible for staging the series of demonstrations required by the succession of company and platoon commanders' courses. Once a year, as the climax of the training season, they produced the actors for the annual demonstration, the show-piece of the School.

To cater for these demands they were reorganized into two rifle companies, responsible for the demonstrations, and Training and Headquarters and Support companies. The programme was quite rigid and the Battalion's commitments were known well ahead. To ensure smooth co-operation between the School and the Battalion, a liaison officer worked permanently at the School headquarters. This role was an important one; it was initially held by Major Burgess and later by Major Bush. When warned by the liaison officer of exactly what was wanted, the appropriate company, under the eyes of the School staff, would rehearse until it was perfect and on the actual day would carry out such last-minute adjustments, for example, ranging, as were necessary. The actual demonstrations were not unpopular with the men who by no means disliked acting the part of 'dead' or 'wounded'. Continuity was, by and large, provided by the sergeants who changed less than the officers and men. Long before the date of the annual demonstration all normal courses ceased and everything was devoted to the impeccable production of this great display of infantry tactics, equipment and ideas. In fact, despite the introduction of remarks on nuclear war in the commentaries, the actual Infantrymen carried on much the same as before.

On 26 April 1958 Lieutenant-Colonel Baily handed over command to Lieutenant-Colonel W. R. Lawson. It is unlikely that any commanding officer of the Regiment in time of peace has had to contend with so many moves as has Colonel Baily, starting with his battalion scattered over the wilds of Pahang, coping with the appallingly difficult moves of the Suez Crisis and ending in the quiet of Warminster. He was undoubtedly lucky in having such a resourceful Quartermaster as Major T. Meredith, who proved well capable of dealing with the constant moving and frequent dispersion by companies. At his final parade at Knook Camp, Lieutenant-Colonel Baily asked how many men had been in Pahang when he assumed command: some ten hands were raised. It is this turn-over of men that has been such a problem for commanding officers since the war.

On 3 November 1958 the Battalion provided a Guard of Honour for General J. H. N. Poett, the General Officer Commanding Southern Command. A few days later they provided one for the various generals attending the Tripartite Infantry Conference. On 9 January 1959 Lieutenant Lane and R.S.M. Bartlett took a squad to London to give an arms drill display before the Army Council. This was for approval of the new drill made necessary by the introduction of the self-loading rifle. The squad, parading alongside a Foot Guards detachment, made a big impression and doubtless have ensured that Light Infantry drill movements are for ever incorporated in the drill of the future. In July Major Gooch took a party of men to take part in the Bath Tattoo. A display of silent arms drill was particularly popular with the spectators.

About this time the Army, and the infantry in particular, were suffering from considerable moral strain. On the one hand there was the prospect of many regiments being amalgamated, with the consequent surplus of many senior officers and Warrant officers. On the other hand there was the Government's offer of improved retirement terms to those likely to be redundant. For those who could see no future with their Regiment after twenty or more years' service with it, it was a hard decision to cast aside their careers as soldiers and launch themselves into the civilian jungle. It was a worrying time for all and there were deep stresses beneath the surface.

But the sands were running out for the Regiment as the 1st Battalion made the final preparations for the Farewell Parade and Regimental Reunion to be held at Knook Camp on 12 September 1959. It was fitting that the stage management of this final parade should be in the hands of R.S.M.

Bartlett, M.B.E., M.S.M. After twelve years as Regimental Sergeant-Major of the 1st Battalion it was an appropriate, though sad, climax to his career with the Regiment. His first big parade had been that for the evacuation of India; this was his last.

During 1959 officers from the Duke of Cornwall's Light Infantry began to be posted to the Battalion, while Somerset officers went to join the 1st Battalion the Duke of Cornwall's Light Infantry in Germany. It was in Germany that the two battalions were to amalgamate under the command of Lieutenant-Colonel W. R. Lawson. There were to be many officers and Non-Commissioned officers unable to find places in the new 1st Battalion the Somerset and Cornwall Light Infantry; some of these chose to retire and some were posted to jobs away from the Regiment.

Coupled with the amalgamation of the two regiments was a reorganization of the training arrangements for the Light Infantry Brigade. In the place of the old regimental depots a Brigade Depot was to be formed, and Shrewsbury was selected as the home of this new training centre. As the King's Shropshire Light Infantry Depot at Shrewsbury could not for some time be enlarged to cater for the increase, the new Regiment was to be allowed to retain its individual Depot for the time being. Of course there could only be one Depot for the new Regiment, and Bodmin was chosen for this temporary role. The old Depot of the Somerset Light Infantry was to become the Regimental Headquarters of the Somerset and Cornwall Light Infantry and so maintain the connection with the County. Later, when the Bodmin Depot would have been incorporated into the Light Infantry Depot at Shrewsbury, a small staff would remain at Bodmin to maintain the Cornish connection. All these changes were to take place as soon as possible after the amalgamation of the two 1st Battalions.

And so, on 12 September 1959, came the last day of the history of the Somerset Light Infantry. It was a fine Autumn day; the sun shone; tents lined the parade ground; the

Wiltshire Downs girdled the scene. From all over England came former members of the Regiment with their families: over one thousand were present. It was a Regimental occasion and there were no official guests. The 1st Battalion paraded in impeccable ceremonial order for inspection by the Colonel of the Regiment, Field-Marshal Lord Harding. The Colours were trooped; the Parade advanced in Review order; the Field-Marshal addressed them, the tenor of his speech being: 'The spirit will live on'. The Battalion then marched past in quick and slow time, finally marching off to the strains of *Auld Lang Syne*. And then paraded the Old Comrades, the medals of many campaigns on their breasts, for inspection by the Colonel of the Regiment. Again the Regimental March rang out, as these former warriors marched past at Light Infantry pace applauded by the young men of the Battalion —a moving tribute from the present to the past. Later came a Ceremonial Guard Mounting parade followed by the band and bugles sounding Retreat. The gathering then broke up to exchange hospitality in the various messes, but all were present for what was possibly the most poignant moment of a memorable day: at eleven o'clock the host of watchers, while listening to the silvery notes of 'Last Post' ringing hauntingly over the camp, saw the Regimental Badge, illuminated on the Downs above, plunged in darkness.

And the spirit *will* live on. Two hundred and seventy-four years of history is not extinguished while there are men to carry on. The new regiment is there to carry the traditions, the pride and the burdens into the future, the Territorials are a present force, the Association is the repository of the past.

The following were the principal office-holders on the day of the Farewell Parade:

Commanding Officer .	Lieutenant-Colonel W. R. Lawson, M.B.E.	
Second-in-command .	Major J. T. C. Howard, M.C. (D.C.L.I.)	
Adjutant . . .	Captain D. H. McMurtrie	

Quartermaster . .	Major T. Meredith, M.B.E.
R.S.M. . . .	R.S.M. K. E. Bartlett, M.B.E., M.S.M.
	O.R.Q.M.S. C. Clark
	R.Q.M.S. R. G. Gillard
A Company . .	Major P. F. Gooch
	C.S.M. P. Smyth
B Company . .	Major T. G. Alexander (D.C.L.I.)
	C.S.M. C. E. K. Driver
Headquarter Company (One Group) . .	Major M. C. Watts C.S.M. A. A. Lynas-Gray
Headquarter Company (Two Group) . .	Major F. J. Cooke-Hurle C.S.M. A. Morris
Liaison officer with School of Infantry .	Major P. J. Bush
Battalion Paymaster .	Major G. J. Palmer (R.A.P.C.)
Reunion officer . .	Major S. R. W. Slinger
Bandmaster . .	Mr N. F. Hirst

ROLL OF HONOUR

MALAYA

Captain Dennis Graham Lock. 2 October 1949. Killed in action with 2nd Battalion, King's Own Yorkshire Light Infantry.

Private Robert John Clare. 5 December 1952. Accidentally killed.

Private Edward William Victor Pheasant. 18 January 1953. Accidentally killed.

Sergeant Raymond Beaumont. 27 January 1953. Killed in action.

Corporal David Martin Clothier. 29 January 1953. Killed in action.

Private Alan Keith Johnson. 7 February 1953. Killed in action.

Lance-Corporal Eric John Down. 29 April 1953. Died.

Lieutenant John Rupert Stephen Mather. 26 June 1953. Killed with 3rd King's African Rifles.

Private Gerald John Cox. 14 December 1953. Died.

Private Graham Frederick Cleveland. 29 December 1953. Accidentally killed.

Private Wyndham Barry Matthews. 13 February 1954. Accidentally killed.

Private James Arthur Leeworthy. 21 February 1954. Died.

Private Brian William George Plympton. 8 July 1954. Died.

Private Brian William Peter Spurr. 11 July 1954. Accidentally killed.

Corporal George Shaw. 21 February 1955. Killed in action.

Second Lieutenant Benjamin Heath. 15 March 1955. Killed in action.

Sergeant Michael Joseph Hanlan. 23 April 1955. Killed in action.

Lance-Corporal Edward George Martin. 28 April 1955. Died.

Private Anthony Brian Bennett. 29 May 1955. Killed in action.

Private Glynn Bessant. 24 June 1955. Died in action.

Lance-Corporal Anthony Charles Henry Farrance. 25 August 1955. Died.

SUEZ

Corporal George Crawford. 6 November 1956. Killed in action.

HONOURS AND AWARDS GRANTED TO MEMBERS OF THE REGIMENT
1946–1960

1st Battalion—Malaya

M.B.E.
Major J. J. Ogilvie
Major R. H. D. Norman, M.C.
Bandmaster W. H. Moore, A.R.C.M.

M.C.
Second Lieutenant R. A. Douglas
Major P. Haigh

M.M.
Company Sergeant-Major R. A. Puddy
Corporal D. I. Clements
Corporal J. L. F. Ballantyne
Private F. G. Davis

Mentioned in Despatches
Lieutenant-Colonel V. S. Baily
Major J. R. Burgess, M.B.E.
Major R. J. Stevens
Major K. J. Whitehead, M.C.
Major J. L. Waddy
Captain C. D. C. Frith
Captain D. R. Goddard
Captain G. G. Thomas (R.A.M.C.)
Lieutenant R. E. Waight
Lieutenant R. W. Houghton
Lieutenant A. C. W. Mitford-Slade
Lieutenant D. R. McMurtrie
Lieutenant K. J. Shapland

Lieutenant E. D. Capper
Lieutenant O. J. M. Eley
Lieutenant E. G. Longman
Regimental Sergeant-Major K. E. Bartlett
Company Sergeant-Major A. J. Longney
Company Sergeant-Major R. Harton (K.S.L.I.)
Colour-Sergeant H. Bone
Colour-Sergeant M. W. Worle
Colour-Sergeant R. G. Gillard
Sergeant R. W. Bellringer
Sergeant Bruce (R.E.M.E.)
Sergeant R. C. B. Cox
Sergeant D. J. Cridge
Sergeant E. W. Herrington
Sergeant J. M. O'Reilly, D.C.M.
Sergeant M. A. Soloman
Sergeant J. M. Lowery
Sergeant Winrow (K.O.Y.L.I.)
Corporal R. Abernathy
Corporal J. D. Eade
Corporal W. A. Melluish
Lance-Corporal Sinclair
Lance-Corporal Angkin anah Ngerubbne (Iban)

Commander-in-Chief's Certificate
Sergeant Everington (R.E.M.E.)
Corporal Greenman
Lance-Corporal Ballard
Corporal Dari anah Nyabong (Iban)
Lance-Corporal Baroah anah Nyipa (Iban)
Lance-Corporal Kayan anah Tungan (Iban)

Other Awards

1946–60

Baron
Field-Marshal Sir John Harding, G.C.B., C.B.E., D.S.O., M.C.

G.C.B.

General Sir John Harding, K.C.B., C.B.E., D.S.O., M.C.

C.B.

Major-General C. L. Firbank, C.B.E., D.S.O.

C.B.E.

Major-General C. L. Firbank, D.S.O.
Major-General R. H. Barry, O.B.E.
Brigadier J. F. Snow
Colonel W. Q. Roberts, D.S.O., M.V.O., T.D., J.P., A.D.C.
Brigadier C. S. Howard, D.S.O., O.B.E.

O.B.E.

Lieutenant-Colonel W. Q. Roberts, D.S.O., T.D.
Lieutenant-Colonel C. J. Stewart, T.D.
Lieutenant-Colonel E. A. Trotman, T.D.

M.B.E.

Major W. R. Lawson
Captain T. Meredith
Major J. R. Burgess
Major J. A. H. Clarke
Regimental Sergeant-Major H. E. Knight (with K.S.L.I.)
Regimental Sergeant-Major K. E. Bartlett
Regimental Quartermaster-Sergeant H. C. J. Gray

D.S.O.

Brigadier C. S. Howard, O.B.E.

M.V.O.

Colonel W. Q. Roberts, D.S.O., T.D.

M.C.

Major R. J. Stevens (with Parachute Regiment, Port Said,
    1956)

B.E.M.

Sergeant H. Cotton
Yeoman Clerk L. A. Ellis
Company Sergeant-Major W. R. Tuckfield
Bugle-Major H. E. Wiltshire
Mr. C. Hill

M.S.M.
Warrant Officer (Class 2) F. Hillier
Company Sergeant-Major H. Hucker
Company Sergeant-Major A. J. Longney
Warrant Officer (Class 2) E. T. Mullen
Regimental Sergeant-Major K. E. Bartlett, M.B.E.
Mr C. S. W. Trickey
Mr E. Gibbs
Mr S. J. Rogers
Mr G. Tompkins
Mr C. Hill
Mr W. M. Matthews
Mr R. Cowley
Mr J. S. W. Mounter, M.B.E.
Mr J. Willis

Mentioned in Despatches
Major V. W. Beckhurst, M.C. (with Malay Regiment in Malaya, 1958).
Brigadier C. S. Howard, O.B.E.

AWARD OF THE GEORGE CROSS TO CAPTAIN SIMMON LATUTIN
ON 29 DECEMBER 1944 IN SOMALILAND

Captain Simmon Latutin was the son of two emigrés, a Russian Jew and a Pole. He was born in England. After a musical education and graduating at London University, he became a member of the London Symphony Orchestra. On the outbreak of the Second World War he was called up and, on account of poor eyesight, was posted to the Pioneer Corps. Later, however, he was selected for officer training and, in due course, was commissioned into the Regiment in 1942.

After serving with the 9th Battalion in Northern Ireland he was sent to East Africa in early 1943. It was there, when Commandant of the Somalie Gendarmerie School, that he won the posthumous award of the George Cross on 29 December 1944.

This award was announced in the London Gazette on 10 September 1946. The citation ran as follows:

On December 29, 1944, a fire occurred at the training school store of the Somalie Gendarmerie at Mogadishu, while some Italian rockets and explosives were being taken out destined for another unit about to hold a New Year's entertainment. Captain Latutin, together with one officer, a company sergeant-major and a personal boy were in this store selecting the explosives, the first-named standing in the doorway. For some unexplained cause, a fire started and almost simultaneously a great number of rockets began to explode and burn—there were some 170 cases in the store. With the force of the fire, the store became an inferno of danger. Captain Latutin, regardless of the detonating rockets, the intense heat generated by the fire and the choking clouds of smoke, plunged into the store-room and succeeded in dragging out the officer, who was almost unconscious owing to his burning injuries. By this time Captain Latutin was himself alight but, without an instant's hesitation, he again rushed into this seething holocaust of flames and rescued the company sergeant-major, who by this time, owing to the fierce nature of the fire, was quite naked. The body of the boy was later recovered, but was unrecognizable owing to the charred condition of his corpse.

The heroism of Captain Latutin was superb as he fully realised the acute danger which he must incur in entering the building, ablaze with explosives and flames; his unquenchable determination to succour the injured is evinced by his second entry into the store, though himself and his clothes were already alight. His action was illustrative of the finest degree of British courage and a magnificent example of undaunted selflessness. Captain Latutin died as a result of his injuries on the following day.

Appendix C

CAREERS OF COLONELS OF THE REGIMENT

LIEUTENANT-GENERAL SIR JOHN SWAYNE, K.C.B., C.B.E.

Sir John Swayne was educated at Charterhouse and at Trinity College, Oxford. As a university candidate for a commission, he was attached to the 1st Battalion the Somerset Light Infantry at Portland in 1909. On graduating in 1911, he was gazetted to the Regiment and joined the 1st Battalion at Bordon. In August 1914 he went to France as the signals officer of 14th Infantry Brigade and took part in the fighting at Mons. He had the misfortune to be captured at the Battle of Le Cateau. After the war he rejoined the 1st Battalion in Ireland. Apart from a spell as A.D.C. to General Sir Walter Braithwaite in India, he continued to serve with the 1st Battalion until 1925. In 1924 he was appointed Adjutant and at this time qualified as first-class interpreter in French. In 1925 he was a student at the Staff College, Camberley, and on graduating was appointed to the War Office. In 1929 he was Brigade-Major to the 7th Infantry Brigade, then carrying out experiments in mechanization. In 1931 he was appointed Military Assistant to the Chief of the Imperial General Staff. In 1934 he became a student at the Imperial Defence College, but just before the end of the course he was hurried out to the Saar as Chief of Staff to the International Force responsible for law and order during the plebiscite. In April 1935 he was promoted brevet-colonel and after a short stay with the 2nd Battalion at Colchester was selected to command the 1st Battalion the Northumberland Fusiliers in Egypt. In 1937 he was appointed G.S.O.I. at the Staff College, Camberley, and in 1939 became chief instructor at the newly formed Senior Staff College at Minley.

On the outbreak of the Second World War, he was appointed head of the British Military Mission to the French G.Q.G. At the fall of France in 1940 he managed to escape after the armistice and return to England where he was appointed D.C.G.S. at Home Forces Headquarters. In October 1940 he was appointed commander of 4th Infantry Division. Early in 1942 he was appointed C.G.S. Home Forces and in October G.O.C.-in-C. of South-Eastern Command, which he commanded until 1944 when he was sent to India as Chief of the General Staff. In 1946 he was selected as Adjutant-General, but ill-health prevented him from taking up this appointment.

It is notable that General Swayne is one of the few officers who, having been a prisoner in the 1914–18 war, rose to the rank of general in the 1939–45 war.

General Swayne was appointed a C.B.E. in 1940, a C.B. in 1942 and a K.C.B. in 1944. He was Colonel of the Regiment from 15 October 1947 until 13 April 1953.

FIELD-MARSHAL THE RIGHT HONOURABLE THE LORD HARDING OF PETHERTON, G.C.B., C.B.E., D.S.O., M.C.

Allan Francis Harding was born at South Petherton, Somerset, on 10 February 1896 and was educated at Ilminster Grammar School. In May 1914 he was commissioned into the 1/11th Battalion The London Regiment. Later he transferred to the Machine-Gun Corps. He saw active service in Gallipoli and in the Palestine campaign. During the First World War he was awarded the M.C., was mentioned in despatches, commanded a battalion of the Machine-Gun Corps and, when barely twenty years of age, commanded a brigade until wounded. He was granted a Regular commission in the Somerset Light Infantry to date from March 1917. In 1922 he was Adjutant of the 2nd Battalion in India. After graduating from the Staff College in 1930, he held staff appointments at Southern Command, at Catterick, with the International Force in the Saar and at the War Office. In 1939 he assumed command of the 1st Battalion in India, and led them into action on the North-west Frontier: he was mentioned in despatches.

In September 1939 he was sent to Egypt, where he held a series of appointments of ever-increasing importance. He was successively G.S.O.I. 6th Division, B.G.S. Western Desert Force, B.G.S. 13th Corps, D.M.T. Middle East, D.C.G.S. Middle East. In September 1942 he took command of the 7th Armoured Division, which he led from El Alamein until, in January 1943, he was severely wounded in his tank outside Tripoli. On recovering from his wounds, he was promoted to lieutenant-general and was appointed to command 8th Corps in England, but almost at once he was sent to Italy to become C.G.S. 15th Army Group. In December 1944 he became Chief of Staff to the Supreme Commander, Central Mediterranean Forces. In March 1945 he was commanding 13th Corps and was responsible for the handling of the delicate Trieste negotiations at the end of hostilities.

After the Second World War he held most of the major commands, before becoming Chief of the Imperial General Staff. He was G.O.C.-in-C. Central Mediterranean Forces until, in July 1947, he returned to England as G.O.C.-in-C. Southern Command. In July 1949 he was sent as Commander-in-Chief Far East Land Forces; in August 1951 he became Commander-in-Chief British Army of the Rhine. In November 1952 he was appointed Chief of the Imperial General Staff and on retirement in September 1955 was sent by the Government to deal with the Cyprus situation as Governor and Commander-in-Chief. He finally retired from government service in 1957.

He was made a Field-Marshal on 21 July 1953, and was Colonel of the Regiment from 13 April 1953 until its amalgamation with the Duke of Cornwall's Light Infantry in September 1959. He was the first Colonel of the newly formed Somerset and Cornwall Light Infantry. He is also Colonel of the Life Guards, Gold Stick-in-Waiting, and of the 6th Gurkha Rifles.

For his war services he was awarded the D.S.O. with two bars and appointed a C.B.E. In 1944 he was created a K.C.B. and on being knighted obtained the King's permission to be known as Sir John. He was created a G.C.B. in 1951 and was raised to the peerage with the title of Lord Harding of Petherton in 1958. His foreign awards include the Ameri-

Regimental Sergeant-Major K. E. Bartlett, M.B.E., M.S.M.

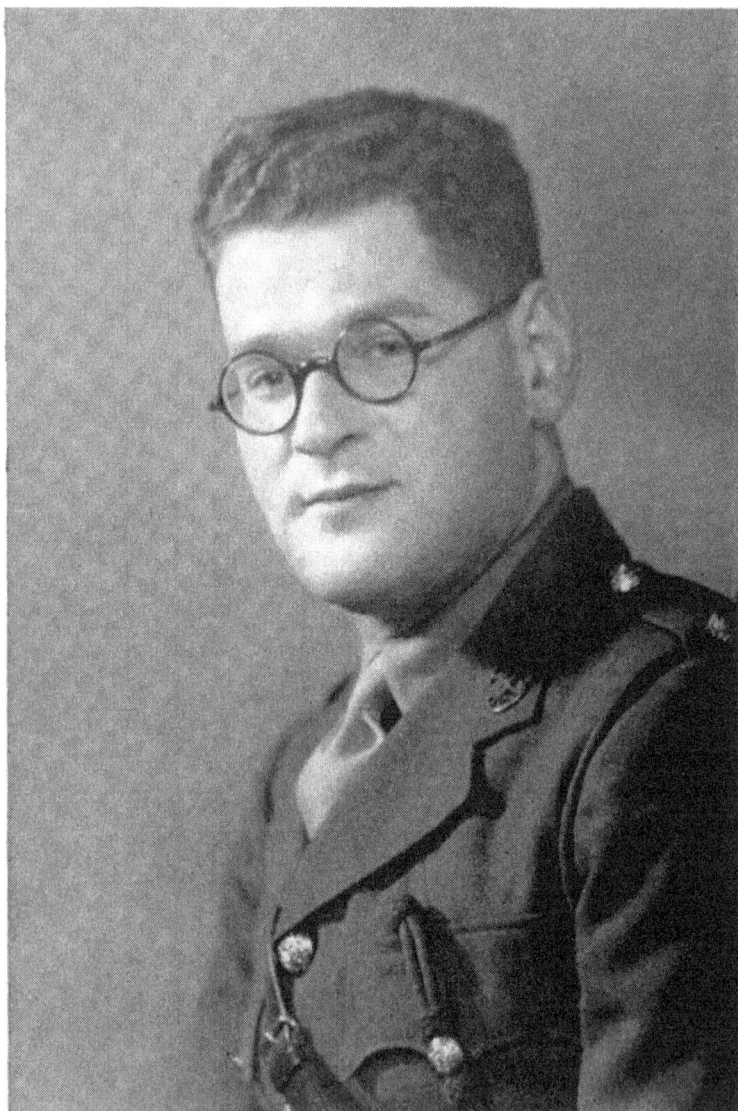

Captain Simmon Latutin, G.C.

can Legion of Merit, the French Legion of Honour and Croix de Guerre. He is also a Knight of the Order of Saint John of Jerusalem.

Appendix D

CAREERS OF SENIOR OFFICERS OF THE REGIMENT

MAJOR-GENERAL CECIL LLEWELLYN FIRBANK, C.B., C.B.E., D.S.O.

General Firbank was educated at Cheltenham College and at Sandhurst. He was commissioned into the Regiment in 1924 and served with the 1st Battalion in England and Egypt until 1929. He was then seconded to the Royal West African Frontier Force, with which he served until 1934, and in which he was adjutant of the 2nd Battalion the Nigerian Regiment. He rejoined the Regiment in 1934 and served with the 2nd Battalion at Colchester, until in 1937 he went as adjutant to the 4th Battalion. On the outbreak of the Second World War he became second-in-command of the 4th Battalion with which he served until 1942, when he was promoted lieutenant-colonel in command of the 6th Battalion of the Regiment. On the disbandment of this battalion, he went to Normandy and assumed command of the 2nd Battalion the Lincolnshire Regiment which he commanded in Normandy, Belgium, Holland and Germany. Later he was promoted to command the 71st Infantry Brigade in the 53rd Welsh Division and, after the end of hostilities, the 160th (South Wales) Infantry Brigade.

In 1947 he went as a student to the Staff College, Camberley, after which he was appointed Commandant of the School of Infantry at Warminster where he remained until 1951. He was then promoted major-general and took over command of the 43rd Division and South-Western District at Taunton. He left Taunton in 1954 to become Director of Infantry at the War Office, during the reorganization of the Infantry, serving there until 1958. He retired in 1959 and was later appointed Chairman of the Somerset Territorial and Auxiliary Forces.

He was awarded the D.S.O. in 1944 and again in 1945. He was made a C.B.E. in 1951 and a C.B. in 1953. He is a Deputy Lieutenant of the County. He has been Honorary Colonel of the 4th/5th Battalion of the Regiment and of the North Somerset Yeomanry (44th Royal Tank Regiment). He is Colonel Commandant of the Aden Protectorate Levies. He acted as Deputy Colonel of the Regiment during Lord Harding's governorship of Cyprus and is now Associate Colonel of the Somerset and Cornwall Light Infantry.

MAJOR-GENERAL CHRISTOPHER GODFREY LIPSCOMB, D.S.O.

Major-General Lipscomb was educated at Charterhouse and Sandhurst. He was commissioned into the Regiment in 1928. From 1933 to 1939 he was seconded to the Nigerian Regiment of the West African Frontier Forces. During the Second World War he took over command of the 4th Battalion of the Regiment directly they landed in Normandy and continued to command them throughout the whole European campaign with outstanding distinction.

After the war he went as a student to the Staff College and, on graduation, went to Taunton as a Staff officer on the Headquarters of the 43rd Division. In 1950 he was promoted brigadier and assumed command of the 19th Infantry Brigade which he commanded in England and Egypt until 1953. He was then appointed Commandant of the Senior Officers' School. In 1957 he went to Germany as Commander Hanover District. In 1958 he was appointed Chief of the Joint Services Liaison Organization in the British Army of the Rhine.

He was awarded the D.S.O. and a Bar during 1945.

MAJOR-GENERAL RICHARD HUGH BARRY, C.B.E.

General Barry was educated at Winchester and Sandhurst. He was commissioned into the Regiment in 1929. In 1935 he was an instructor at the Small Arms School, Netheravon. In 1938 he graduated at the Staff College and was then appointed Brigade-Major to the 13th Infantry Brigade. On the outbreak of the Second World War he was posted to the General Headquarters of the British Expeditionary Force in

France. In 1940 he was at the War Office and at Minley
Senior Staff College. In 1941 he was again at the War Office
in Military Intelligence, having been promoted lieutenant-
colonel. In 1942 he was on the Staff of the Allied Forces
Headquarters in Algiers. He returned to the War Office in
1943, again on the Intelligence Staff, as a colonel. In 1945
he became the Deputy Director of Plans. He went to Stock-
holm as Military Attaché in 1947, and in 1948 was the
Deputy Chief of Staff at Western European Land Forces
Headquarters. In 1950 he was posted to the Ministry of
Defence on the Joint Planning Staff and in 1951 he went
to Washington on the Joint Services Mission. In 1952 he
became the Director of the Standing Group at the North
Atlantic Treaty Organization. From 1954 to 1956 he was
Chief of Staff of the Headquarters of British Troops Egypt.
He was a student at the Imperial Defence College in 1957
and in 1959 was promoted major-general and assumed an
appointment at the North Atlantic Council.

He was made an O.B.E. in 1943 and a C.B.E. in 1953.

BRIGADIER JOHN ROWLEY INNES PLATT, D.S.O.

Brigadier Platt was educated at Wellington College and
at the Royal Military College, Sandhurst. He was commissioned into the Regiment in 1925 serving with the 1st Battalion in India, of which he was adjutant from 1931 to 1934.
From 1935 to 1937 he attended the Staff College, Quetta and,
on graduating, was appointed Brigade-Major to the Army
Gas School. The outbreak of the Second World War found
him in France on the staff of 1st Corps and in the evacuation
of Dunkirk. Subsequently he was Brigade-Major of 5th
Infantry Brigade and then second-in-command successively
of the 7th Battalion of the Regiment and of the 1st Buckinghamshire Battalion of the Oxford and Buckinghamshire
Light Infantry. In 1942 he went to North Africa on the staff
of 1st Army and then served in 18th Army Group and in
Tunisia and Sicily. After a very brief period as commandant
of the Army Gas School in England, he went to Gibraltar
to take command of the 2nd Battalion, which he took to

Egypt for training and then led into action in Italy. He was seriously wounded at the crossing of the River Garigliano, when in temporary command of the brigade. When he had recovered from his wounds he was at the War Office and then on the Staff of 2nd Army in Germany. He also commanded the 5th Battalion of the Regiment preparing for the war in the Far East, but the war ended before it could be used.

After the war he was sent to Washington as a colonel on the British Army Staff before going to India to command the 1st Battalion when that country was evacuated. From 1948 to 1949 he was at the School of Infantry. In 1950 he was promoted brigadier and took command of 130th Infantry Brigade, Territorial Army, in which was the 4th/5th Battalion, at Exeter. He retired in 1952 and has since then been Secretary of the Wiltshire Territorial and Auxiliary Forces Association.

He was awarded the D.S.O. in 1944 and mentioned in despatches in 1943.

Brigadier John Fitzgerald Snow, C.B.E.

Brigadier Snow was educated at Wellington College and the Royal Military College, Sandhurst. On commissioning into the Regiment, he joined the 1st Battalion at Devonport before going to the 2nd Battalion at Khartoum. He returned with the 2nd to England and was stationed at Tidworth and Blackdown until in 1934 he went to Poona to join the 1st Battalion. From 1935 to 1936 he was at the Depot, and from 1937 to 1938 at the Staff College, Camberley. On graduation, he was posted as Brigade-Major of the 10th Infantry Brigade, initially at Shorncliffe, and then in France. During 1940–43 he was in succession an instructor at the Senior Officers' School, a G.S.O.I. in the North of England, in Northern Ireland, at the War Office and second-in-command 7th South Staffordshire Regiment. In 1943 he went to the Far East as a staff officer at South-East Asia Command. In 1944 he became Second-in-command of the 1st Northamptonshire Regiment in India before taking command of the 1st Devonshire

Regiment in Burma. In 1946 he was on the staff of an Area in India before returning to Europe to take over command of the 2nd Battalion in Greece in 1947, taking them first to Austria and then back to England. He was the first commander of the amalgamated 1st and 2nd Battalions, when the Regiment took over the duties of Light Infantry Training Centre. In 1949 he was appointed Garrison Commander Benghazi as a colonel, where he served until 1952. On promotion to brigadier, he was appointed Deputy Commander of the Fortress of Gibraltar, which was his last appointment before retirement.

He was appointed a C.B.E. in 1956 and was mentioned in despatches in 1940 and 1946.

BRIGADIER CHARLES STORRS HOWARD, C.B.E., D.S.O.

Brigadier Howard was educated at Haileybury College and at the Royal Military College, Sandhurst. He was commissioned into the Regiment in 1926 and was adjutant of the 1st Battalion in India from 1934 to 1937. During the Second World War he commanded the 5th Battalion of the Regiment in England and Ireland from 1942 until 1944. He was then flown out to India to assume command of the 1st Battalion, which was then preparing to return to Burma. He continued to command this battalion until 1947, when he went to the Staff College, Quetta. After graduating he held various staff appointments in England before returning to command the 1st Battalion again at Bordon and later in Germany. In 1952 he was promoted brigadier and went out to Malaya to command the 26th Gurkha Infantry Brigade which he continued to do until 1955. He then became Deputy Director of Military Training at the War Office until he retired in 1958. Since retiring he has run the Army Outward Bound School in Wales.

He was awarded the D.S.O. in 1954 and made a C.B.E. in 1959. He was mentioned in despatches in 1953.

BRIGADIER JAMES LINDESAY BRIND, D.S.O.

Brigadier Brind was educated at Wellington College and at the Royal Military College, Sandhurst. He was commissioned into the Regiment in 1929 and served with the 2nd Battalion in England before being appointed adjutant of the Depot in 1936. In 1938 he joined the 1st Battalion at Poona, with whom he remained until returning to England in 1940. He graduated at the Staff College, Camberley, in 1943 and was then appointed to the Headquarters of the 38th Infantry Division. Soon after D Day in 1944 he went to Normandy and became Second-in-command of the 4th Battalion, with whom he served until he was appointed to command the 5th Battalion the Wiltshire Regiment for the Rhine Crossing. When 5th Wiltshires were disbanded he took command of the 4th Devons. From 1946 until 1948 he was on the staff of the School of Infantry at Warminster and then went to Egypt at Middle East Land Forces Headquarters. In 1952 he took over command of the 1st Battalion in Germany and took them to Malaya. In 1955 he was promoted brigadier and assumed command of the 159th Infantry Brigade of the Territorial Army. In 1958 he went to Germany as Deputy Commander, Rhine Army District and later became Commander of Rhine Area. He was awarded the D.S.O. in 1946.

Appendix E

SUCCESSION OF LIEUTENANT-COLONELS COMMANDING BATTALIONS
1946–1960

1st Battalion

C. S. Howard . .	June 1944—February 1947
J. R. I. Platt . .	July 1947—March 1948

2nd Battalion

A. Hunt . . .	January—December 1946
J. F. Snow . .	January 1947—June 1948

1st Battalion

J. F. Snow . .	June 1948—June 1949
C. S. Howard . .	June 1949—April 1952
J. L. Brind . .	April 1952—March 1955
V. S. Baily . .	March 1955—April 1958
W. R. Lawson . .	April 1958—September 1959

4th Battalion

W. Q. Roberts . .	April 1947—April 1952
C. J. Stewart . .	May 1952—April 1955
E. A. Trotman . .	May 1955—April 1958
T. H. Harding . .	May 1958 onwards

Appendix F

SUCCESSION OF DEPOT COMMANDERS
1946–1960

A. Hunt . . .	April—December 1948 (previously commanded 13th Primary Training Centre)
P. Lewis . . .	December 1948—October 1951
J. H. G. Wells . .	October 1951—October 1952
C. C. A. Carfrae .	October 1952—December 1955
T. M. Braithwaite .	December 1955—September 1958
C. W. E. Satterthwaite	September 1958—September 1959

Appendix G

SUCCESSION OF ADJUTANTS
1946–1960

1st Battalion

G. W. Stead	.	October 1945—May 1946
P. J. Bush	.	June 1946—May 1947
E. J. Kingston	.	June—October 1947
F. M. De Butts	.	October 1947

(vacancy until amalgamation of 1st and 2nd in June 1948)

2nd Battalion

T. L. Ingram	.	March—October 1946
E. A. Sutton-Pryce	.	November 1946—September 1947
R. G. Woodhouse	.	September 1947—April 1948
P. Haigh	.	April—June 1948

1st Battalion

P. Haigh	.	June—November 1948
R. J. Stevens	.	November 1948—February 1950
P. J. Bush	.	February 1950—January 1952
A. J. Collyns	.	January 1952—December 1953
C. D. C. Frith	.	January 1954—June 1956
R. B. Robertson	.	June 1956—July 1958
D. R. McMurtrie	.	July 1958—October 1959
B. M. Lane	.	October 1959—amalgamation

Depot

H. Platt	.	April—September 1948 ⎫ Appointed as Depot Captains
D. J. Boughton	.	October—December 1948 ⎬
M. C. Watts	.	January 1949—August 1951 ⎭
R. G. Woodhouse	.	August 1951—September 1953
P. N. Pearson	.	October 1953—November 1954
S. R. W. Slinger	.	November 1954—April 1956

138

Depot (continued)

W. H. White	. .	April 1956—April 1958
J. F. A. Overton	.	April 1958—October 1959

4th Battalion

G. W. Stead	. .	March 1947—March 1950
R. G. Stevens	.	March—December 1950
T. M. Braithwaite	.	December 1950—October 1952
M. J. Ryall	.	October 1952—October 1954
R. E. Waight	.	November 1954—March 1957
J. M. S. Thain	. .	March 1957—March 1958
G. J. Duckworth	.	March 1958 onwards

Appendix H

SUCCESSION OF QUARTERMASTERS
1946–1960

1st Battalion

C. W. Smart	. .	June 1943—May 1947
W. J. Atkins	. .	May 1947—June 1948

2nd Battalion

J. S. Cavanagh	. .	April 1944—July 1946
J. W. Grant	. .	August 1946—April 1948
G. H. Farmer	. .	April—June 1948

1st Battalion

G. H. Farmer	. .	June 1948—March 1949
R. P. H. Fortnum	.	April 1949—December 1951
C. W. Smart	. .	December 1951—August 1954
T. Meredith	. .	September 1954 to amalgamation

Depot

C. W. Smart	. .	May 1947—March 1949
G. H. Farmer	. .	April 1949—January 1952
R. P. H. Fortnum	.	February 1952—October 1954
C. W. Smart	. .	October 1954—February 1959
M. Scott	. . .	February 1959 to closure

4th Battalion

L. F. Male	. .	March—July 1947
R. P. H. Fortnum	.	July 1947—March 1949
C. W. Smart	. .	March 1949—December 1951
M. Scott	. . .	December 1951—February 1959
A. F. Frost	. .	February 1959 onwards

Appendix J

SUCCESSION OF REGIMENTAL SERGEANT-MAJORS
1946–1960

1st Battalion

T. J. Land .	. 1946 (acting)
W. Canniford .	. 1946 (acting)
C. E. Sampson .	. October 1946—April 1947 (acting)
A. J. Longney .	. April 1947—January 1948 (acting)
K. E. Bartlett .	. January 1948—April 1948

2nd Battalion

R. Baldwin .	. 1946 (acting)
R. Gillard .	. 1946—1947 (acting)
S. Smale . .	. 1947—April 1948 (acting)

1st Battalion

S. Smale . .	. April 1948—February 1949
K. E. Bartlett, M.B.E., M.S.M. . . .	February 1949—October 1959

Depot

H. Smith, M.B.E. .	January—March 1947 (13th P.T.C.)
E. Gibbs . . .	March 1947—June 1948 (13th P.T.C.)
H. E. Knight, M.B.E.	July—August 1948 (then to K.S.L.I.)
J. S. W. Mounter, M.B.E. . . .	August 1948—August 1953
C. E. Sampson . .	August 1953—September 1957
A. V. Worster . .	September 1957—October 1959

4th Battalion

W. L. C. Tilley . .	May 1947—January 1952
H. Gray . . .	April 1952—March 1954
F. C. Perkins . .	March 1954—February 1955
F. Fouracre . .	February 1955—January 1960
A. V. Worster . .	January 1960 onwards

Appendix K

THE ROYAL HAMILTON LIGHT INFANTRY
(The Wentworth Regiment)

In the year 1862 the town of Hamilton in Ontario was authorized to raise a regiment of Militia. This was the XIIIth Regiment and is the ancestor of the regiment now known as the Royal Hamilton Light Infantry. It has variously been known as the Royal Battalion, the Royal Regiment, and the Royal Hamilton Regiment. The additional title comes from the Wentworth Regiment, with whom it was amalgamated in 1936. It was affiliated to the Somerset Light Infantry in 1910. Luckily Canada is sufficiently close for personal contacts between members of both Regiments to take place with some frequency. In its original form it was raised to guard the frontier with the United States of America, at that time liable to be troubled. In those days all able-bodied men automatically belonged, only being paid when actually on duty. It has always been an entirely volunteer force.

It was during the South African War that members of the Regiment volunteered for the first time to serve abroad, and were in the force that Canada sent to help the United Kingdom against the Boers. During the First World War it took a prominent part in the fighting in Flanders. During the Second World War the Regiment was part of the heroic force that took part in the Dieppe Raid and suffered appalling casualties. Later it took part in the North-West European Campaign, fighting at Caen, at the Falaise Gap, at Antwerp, in the Rhineland and at the crossing of the Rhine. At different times during this war the Royal Hamilton Light Infantry were able to meet members of the Territorial Battalions of the Somerset Light Infantry in England and in Germany. Since the war it has become closely connected with the problems of civil defence against atomic attack.

Royal Hamilton Light Infantry

The town of Hamilton is some forty miles from the Niagara Falls. Its Armouries in the town are large enough to house two battalions on parade, which may make English Territorials a bit jealous. It is a very keen shooting regiment and annually sends a team to Bisley. It is extremely proud of its bugle band which is, in fact, a silver trumpet band: its bugles are only blown on special occasions. It is an extremely democratic force and any rank may be held by the members of one family: private, sergeant-major or colonel. Its most illustrious member was the late Major-General the Honourable S. C. Mewburn, K.C., P.C., C.M.G., V.D.D., who started as a private and ended by holding the post of Minister of Militia and Defence.

In recent years much has been seen of members of the Royal Hamilton Light Infantry in connection with the official unveiling of their Memorial at Dieppe and various pilgrimages to it by the survivors.

Appendix L

THE MACQUARIE REGIMENT

THE Australian XIIIth Infantry Battalion was first raised in September 1914 in Sydney, New South Wales. It formed part of the first Australian contingent to come to the help of the mother country during the First World War.

After a brief stay in Egypt the XIIIth Battalion took part in the assault-landing on Anzac beach in the Dardanelles. Landing on 25 April 1915 they remained on the peninsula throughout all the subsequent bitter fighting until it was evacuated in December 1915. By July 1916 they were in Flanders and from then on until the end of the war took part in all the major offensives. During this war they produced two distinguished Australian soldiers: Brigadier S. C. E. Herring, C.M.G., D.S.O., and Major-General A. S. Allen, C.B., C.B.E., D.S.O., who was later to command the Australian 7th Division in the Second World War. They also won two Victoria Crosses: Lieutenant-Colonel Harry Murray, V.C., C.M.G., D.S.O. and Bar, D.C.M., and Sergeant Maurice Buckley, V.C., D.C.M. The XIIIth Battalion was disbanded after the war and when it was re-formed it was re-named the Maitland Regiment.

During the Second World War the XIIIth Battalion (The Maitland Regiment) raised two battalions. The 1st XIIIth was used exclusively in Australia on guard and training duties. The 2nd XIIIth saw much active foreign service. In October 1940 it was briefly in India before going on to Egypt in November. In May 1941, moving into the front line, it was cut off after heavy fighting near Tobruk and thereafter became part of the garrison throughout that famous siege. When the siege was lifted in December 1941, it went to Palestine and later to Syria, returning in November 1942 in time to take part in the Battle of El Alamein. Once again it was withdrawn to Palestine to refit before returning to Australia. In Australia it prepared to take part in the Pacific war against the Japanese and on 30 July 1943 it landed at Milne Bay, New Guinea. During 1943–4 it took part in the Battles of Lae and Finshafen and in the advance down the Huon Peninsula. It was then withdrawn to Australia to refit. On 10 June 1945 it returned to the front, landing at Brunei in Borneo, and continued in action in Borneo until the end of hostilities in the Far East on 15 August 1945. On returning to Australia it was disbanded and, when it was re-formed, was re-named the Macquarie Regiment, as the town of Maitland was no longer in its recruiting area. The Macquarie Regiment is a volunteer force.

The original affiliation of the Regiment with the Somerset Light Infantry was made with the XIIIth Battalion of the First World War.

Appendix M

THE DUKE OF CORNWALL'S LIGHT INFANTRY

In the reign of Queen Anne, in the year 1702, a regiment of marines was raised by Colonel Fox. This regiment was to become in the course of time the 32nd Foot, and finally the 1st Battalion the Duke of Cornwall's Light Infantry. Serving with the fleet, it at once sailed to Spain, to take part in an unsuccessful attack on the city of Cadiz and the successful capture of a treasure fleet at Vigo. In 1705 it was part of the force of marines that captured the fortress of Gibraltar and remained as garrison throughout the siege. It then went to Catalonia, to take part in the capture of Barcelona.

In the year 1741 Colonel John Price raised a new regiment, the 57th Foot which, re-numbered the 46th Foot in 1748, eventually became the 2nd Battalion the Duke of Cornwall's Light Infantry. This Regiment had its first engagement against the Highlanders in 1745. In 1758 it was in Canada fighting the French; it suffered heavy casualties in the assault on Fort Ticonderoga and was part of the force that captured Fort Niagara. In 1762 it was sent from Canada to the West Indies where it was engaged in the capture of Martinique and Havannah. In 1775 it was in America again, this time fighting the Americans, and its Light Company were part of the force engaged at Brandywine Creek, from which date the red feathers, now the red patch, on the cap badge. In 1782 it was again in the West Indies for the capture of Saint Lucia.

Meanwhile the 32nd Foot had been fighting in Europe in the War of the Austrian Succession, taking part in the battles of Dettingen and Fontenoy in 1743 and in the battle of Lauffeld in 1748.

In 1782, when regiments were first given county connections, the 32nd Foot became the Cornwall Regiment and the 46th the South Devonshire Regiment.

In 1796 both the 32nd and 46th were in the West Indies, the 32nd capturing Saint Domingo, and the 46th fighting the insurgent Caribs in Saint Vincent and Jamaica. Losses from sickness and from the enemy was so great that the 46th had to return to England to rehabilitate themselves. In 1805 they were at the capture of Dominica and in 1810 at the capture of Martinique and Guadeloupe. Meanwhile the 32nd was heavily engaged in Europe against the Napoleonic armies. In 1808 they took part in the battles of Rolica and Vimiera in Portugal under Sir Arthur Wellesley. In 1809 they were with Sir John Moore in his great march across Napoleon's line of communications, the subsequent retreat to Corunna and the battle fought in defence of the port. Later that year they took part in the disastrous Walcheren expedition. The year 1812 saw them back in the Peninsula under Wellington. They fought at the great victory at Salamanca and the siege of Burgos, and when the victorious army advanced into the south of France, they fought at the battles of the Pyrenees, Nivelle, Nive, and Orthes. In 1815 they were in Sir Thomas Picton's Division on the left of the line at the Battle of Waterloo.

The outbreak of the Sikh War in 1848 found the 32nd in India. They took part in the siege and storming of Mooltan and the Battle of Goojerat. They were still in India at the outbreak of the Indian Mutiny. A detachment of the 32nd, with their families, was in the ill-fated garrison of Cawnpore and were all massacred. The remainder of the Regiment was at Lucknow under Sir John Lawrence and, despite appalling losses, held out for the 140 days' siege of the Residency. The men of the Regiment won four Victoria Crosses during the siege and, as a reward for their heroism, the Regiment was converted into Light Infantry. This event is commemorated annually on 17 November.

In 1854 the 46th took part in the Crimean War. The advance party fought at the Battles of the Alma and Inkerman, and the whole Regiment was present at the final capture of Sevastopol.

In 1877 the 32nd and 46th were linked together as a

result of the Cardwell Reforms and a Depot was opened for both Regiments at Bodmin. In 1881 these two Regiments were merged into one of two battalions, the Duke of Cornwall's Light Infantry.

In 1882 the 2nd Battalion served under Sir Garnet Wolseley in the Egyptian war against Arabi Pasha. They took part in the Battle of Tel-el-Kebir. Later they were part of the expedition that tried to rescue General Gordon at Khartoum. In 1889 they went to South Africa where their charge at the Battle of Paardeberg on 18 February 1900 earned them undying fame. This day has ever since been celebrated by the 2nd Battalion. Meanwhile the 1st Battalion had been engaged in Burma in 1891 and on the North-west Frontier of India in 1897.

On the outbreak of the First World War, the 1st Battalion immediately left for France and were engaged in the early battles of the Marne, Le Cateau and the Aisne. Except for a short stay in Italy, it spent the whole war in France and Flanders, taking part in most of the major battles. The 2nd Battalion was in Hong Kong and was initially required to provide a company of men to serve as marines with the fleet. Arriving in France in 1915, it had severe casualties in the first German gas attack at Ypres. Later it was sent to the Salonika front, where it took part in the final attack that put Bulgaria out of the war. The 1st/4th Battalion saw active service in Mesopotamia and in Palestine. The 1st/5th, 6th, 7th and 10th Battalions all fought in France and Flanders for the greater part of the war. The 8th Battalion fought in France and Flanders before being sent to the Salonika front.

Between the wars the 1st Battalion was in Ireland during the troubles in 1921. The 2nd Battalion helped to put down the Iraq Revolt in 1920.

The Second World War found the 1st Battalion in India. In due course it moved to Iraq and then to Egypt. At once it was thrown into battle to try to help stem the defeat being suffered by the Eighth Army at the Battle of Knightsbridge in the Gazala Line. On 5 June 1942, at Bir el Harmat, it was over-run by German tanks and destroyed. Later, the 6th Battalion was converted into the 1st Battalion, but it did not see action.

The 2nd Battalion was in the British Expeditionary Force that went at once to France. In due course they were involved in the defeat of the allied armies and took part in the fighting around Dunkirk before being evacuated to England. In 1943 this battalion joined the First Army and took part in the campaign in Tunisia. Later it was in the invasion of Sicily and the Italian campaign until the end of the war.

The 5th Battalion was in the 43rd Wessex Division and took part in the fighting in Normandy and the remainder of this successful campaign. Its conduct at Hill 112 in Normandy and at Hoven in the Rhineland was particularly notable.

It is perhaps pertinent for the members of the Somerset and Cornwall Light Infantry to note where and when the Somerset Light Infantry and the Duke of Cornwall's Light Infantry have served together in the past. The 32nd Foot was in Gibraltar when the XIIIth arrived with the relieving force, and both remained for the rest of the siege. Both regiments then went on, under Lord Peterborough, to capture Barcelona. During the War of the Austrian Succession both 32nd and XIIIth fought at the Battles of Dettingen, Fontenoy and Lauffeld.

In the early stages of the Napoleonic wars both the 32nd and 46th took part in the capture of San Domingo, where the XIIIth was also engaged. The XIIIth and 46th were again together, in the Carribean in 1810 for the capture of Martinique and Guadeloupe. In the Indian Mutiny it was General Havelock of the XIIIth who led the first relief force to the help of the 32nd besieged in Lucknow. During the Crimean War the 46th and the XIIIth were present at the final capture of Sevastopol. The 2nd Battalion of both regiments were in South Africa during the Boer War. The 1st Battalions of both regiments took part in the Momand campaign on the North-west Frontier in 1897.

During the First World War both Regiments had very

similar histories. Both 1st Battalions were in the British Expeditionary Force and fought throughout the war in Flanders. The Territorial Battalions were engaged in Mesopotamia and in Palestine. The Service Battalions fought in Flanders. In the Second World War the 5th Battalion the Duke of Cornwall's Light Infantry was with the 4th and 7th Somerset Light Infantry in the 43rd Division fighting alongside one another from Normandy to the Elbe. Thus the past history of the two regiments has been intermittently similar.

Appendix N

THE RAND LIGHT INFANTRY

THE Rand Light Infantry was affiliated to the Duke of Cornwall's Light Infantry in 1930. This Regiment is a citizen force of the Defence Forces of the Union of South Africa. It was first raised in 1905 under the title of the Transvaal Cycle Corps: later it became the Transvaal Motor and Cycle Corps. In 1913 its present name became effective.

There are no permanent force officers and Non-Commissioned officers with the Regiment, which is run by the Volunteer officers themselves in their spare time. Each year young men are called up for two months' training under permanent force instructors. After this initial training they are posted to their citizen units, with whom they have to do three weeks' camp annually for three years.

The Rand Light Infantry saw active service during the Zulu Rebellion in 1906, in the Industrial Strike in 1914 and in German South-west Africa in 1914–15. In the Second World War it was in action in the North African Desert campaigns. It fought at Bardia and at Gazala in 1942. It lost a composite company at the fall of Tobruk and its rearguard withdrawing from Gazala lost heavily. It was particularly prominent during the heavy fighting at the Battle of El Alamein. Later it went to Italy, but arrived too late to take part in the fighting.

H.R.H. Princess Margaret has been Colonel-in-Chief of this regiment since 1947.

Appendix O

THE REGIMENTAL ASSOCIATION

THE Somerset Light Infantry Old Comrades Association was first formed in 1910 by Colonel Henry Everett. This was designed to maintain the corporate spirit of members of the Regiment after their retirement; it was also intended to provide assistance to ex-members of the Regiment who were in distress.

In 1938 this association was re-named the Regimental Association, which had the same object as the Old Comrades. The charter of the association was brought up to date after the war in 1948. It now has various funds from which assistance can be given to those in financial or other troubles. Families and dependents of members of the association can also be cared for. Men out of work can get help in finding employment through their local branches.

The headquarters of the Association is at Taunton, but its strength lies in its branches scattered all over the United Kingdom. This strength was well shown at the final Farewell Parade at Knook Camp on 12 September 1959 when over 1,000 members of the Association were present. The biennial reunion at Taunton is the embodiment of the spirit of these ex-members of the Regiment for whom it meant and still means so much.

Branches of the Association are now in being at Bath, Bristol, Birmingham, Bridgwater, Central Somerset, Chard and District, London, Midsomer Norton, Minehead, Northern Ireland, Southampton, Stoke-sub-Hamdon, Taunton, Wakefield, Yeovil.

It is noteworthy that the Regimental Association and the 4th/5th Battalion will be all that remains of the Regiment after the amalgamation with the Duke of Cornwall's Light Infantry.

Appendix P

THE MUSEUM

AT the end of the Second World War the Regimental Museum was in a poor way. In 1950 Lieutenant-Colonel A. Hunt made great efforts to get it into good shape again. As a result of publicity in the *Light Bob Gazette* many gifts were made to the Museum and it grew rapidly under the care of Mr Rowland. For some time it was hampered by lack of adequate funds to make the necessary alterations for the proper display of its exhibits.

Great efforts were made to acquire the five Victoria Crosses won by members of the Regiment. Eventually they were all displayed in the V.C.s' Corner in the museum. They are the medals of Sergeant William Napier, Private Patrick Carlin, Major W. Knox-Leat, Private T. H. Sage and Lieutenant George Cairns. Colonel Hunt also acquired the original of Lady Butler's painting, *Remnants of an Army*, which was recovered from a basement of the Tate Gallery. The attempts to locate the Attar-dan succeeded, but the trophy itself escaped the Regiment, being presented to the Museum at Sandhurst. The uniform of the late King George VI, which he wore as Colonel-in-Chief of the Regiment, is also in the Museum by permission of Her Majesty Queen Elizabeth, the Queen Mother. Recent additions are displays of trophies from Malaya and Port Said.

It is now a worthy depository of the Regiment's trophies and relics, which can be seen displayed to advantage. In due course it is to be moved from the old keep and will be re-established in Jellalabad House, when the Regimental Headquarters of the Somerset and Cornwall Light Infantry is set up there.

At almost the same date as the closing of the Depot Mr Rowland, its custodian, retired. During his twenty-six years with the Regiment he had become an institution. He joined the Depot in 1933, as officers' mess steward, after serving for twenty-six years with the Army Service Corps. In the course of time he moved almost imperceptibly into the museum, of which he soon became the accepted expert and trusted guardian. Apart from his duties as guardian of the museum, he also assumed custody of the wide range and variety of Regimental and personal property that found its way into his care during the war. The Regiment owes him much in this respect. It was Colonel Hunt and Mr Rowland who built up the museum to its present state. Colonel Urwick is now the custodian.

Appendix Q

THE BAND

DURING the Second World War the bands of Regular battalions were mostly removed from them and, placed in War Office pools, were required to travel and perform at the behest of the various headquarters in whose areas they happened to be. Unfortunately, when the 1st Battalion went to Burma, Mr Moore's band went into action as stretcher-bearers, with the result that, when the Battalion was withdrawn, there were hardly any bandsmen left. Mr Coleman and the 2nd Battalion band remained in Gibraltar when the Battalion went to Italy.

Mr Moore was eventually able to reform his band again from reinforcements, and to remain with the Battalion during its various moves around India. The 2nd Battalion was never to see its own band again. When Mr Coleman eventually brought his band back to the Depot, it was soon sent out to India where, for a short time, both it and the 1st Battalion band were together with the 1st Battalion. Both bands suffered severely from demobilization and by the time the 1st Battalion left India Mr Moore had already returned to England to try to re-form. This lack of a band threw an extra load on the buglers who had somehow to fill the gap.

When the 1st and 2nd Battalions were amalgamated, the new band was under the direction of Mr Moore and with a few exceptions was able to stay with the Battalion. In Malaya, however, after having built up a high reputation on ceremonial and other occasions, its numbers fell so low that it had to be sent home to recruit in 1955; in this it was only moderately successful. There were many reasons for this; quite apart from the attraction of higher civilian rates of pay at a time of full employment, there was the endless post-war movement of battalions that meant, for their accompanying bands, little chance of securing playing-out engagements, and those that they did secure were not particularly re-munerative. From this it followed that bandsmen had little opportunity of augmenting their pay. At the time of the amalgamation of regiments, the War Office announced that in future each brigade was to have a staff band on the lines of the Royal Artillery or the Sappers, but that battalions were to have none. This was most unpopular with the Infantry, who considered that a staff band would so rarely be at the disposal of individual regiments that it would be practically worthless. In fact, this decision was rescinded but while it was in force it had a considerable effect on re-cruiting. Undoubtedly, a staff band would have been a more efficient musical unit, which might well have attracted musi-cians by its higher technical standards, higher remuneration from 'playing-out', and a more stable life. But to achieve this, the band would have had to pay the rarest of visits to the battalions for, were it to visit them as often as they would wish, it would have been constantly on the move, which would have vitiated the advantages.

Soon after the return of the 1st Battalion from Malaya, Mr Moore was promoted and became Director of Music to the Brigade of Gurkhas in Malaya. Unfortunately he died not long after. He had been Bandmaster of the 1st Battalion for twenty years. Amongst other matters he had re-orchestrated the Regimental March. Mr Hirst was the new Bandmaster and, in effect, the last.

In 1954 two marches of great historic interest were found and revived as a result of research carried out by John Deni-son, the Music Director of the Arts Council, who had served with the Regiment during the war with some distinction. In the course of his investigations into the origins of Prince Albert's March, he discovered two other marches belonging to the Regiment: one was a quick step and the other a slow march entitled Prince of Wales or XIIIth March. Both, it must be presumed, date from before the conversion of the Regiment to Light Infantry and are the original marches to which the Regiment marched past, when it was an ordi-nary regiment of foot. The quick step has little musical merit and appears to be a country folk-tune. The slow march, on the other hand, is a very fine piece of music in Handelian style and deserves retention on its musical merit alone. Unfortunately, Prince Albert's March is still of unknown provenance: all that can be said of it with any certainty is that it was the quick step of some Imperial German Jaeger Regiment (the German equivalent of our Light Infantry), but of which regiment will probably never be known.

It is to be hoped that the Somerset and Cornwall Light Infantry will not neglect entirely these three marches and that they will find their place in musical programmes on special occasions connected with the XIIIth.

Since the war, and with the ever closer links between Light Infantry Regiments, the band and bugles have taken part in several notable public ceremonies in co-operation with the bands and bugles of the other Light Infantry Regiments. These events have been, of course, quite separate from any ceremony in which the band and bugles have taken part in a parade with the 1st Battalion, Depot or 4th/5th Battalion. In 1956 they took part in these circumstances, in the Royal Tournament and twice they have participated in the S.S.A.F.A. tournaments at the White City. Only a token force was able to take part in the great parade at Shorncliffe, in celebration of the centenary of the birth of Sir John Moore, as the 1st Battalion was then in Malaya.

Appendix R

THE LIGHT BOB GAZETTE

It was in 1893 that the author of the first volume of the Regimental History, Henry Everett, then a captain and later to be knighted and to become a major-general, started to produce the *Light Bob Gazette*. Earlier there had been other attempts in this line, such as the *Griff*, but Everett's venture was to prove lasting and, except for gaps during both the World Wars, it continued until amalgamation in 1959. In effect it became the War Diary of peace-time soldiering and the present volume of the Regimental History could never have been produced without it.

Major F. M. Turner, who had done his best to fill the gap caused by its cessation during the Second World War with a periodical news-letter, was able to re-start its publication in 1946 in the austere style of post-war days. In 1950 Lieutenant-Colonel Hunt, then a retired officer acting as administrative officer to the Depot, made great efforts to increase circulation in order to make it a financially-paying publication. Not only was circulation increased, but so was the standard of literary content, so that it became a periodical of considerable standing; in this he was materially assisted by T. L. Ingram, C. C. A. Carfrae and D. J. Parker, writers of notable merit, who helped to raise the all-round literary standard. Not only did the quarterly contributions from the various active units achieve an unusual standard of readability, but so also did the various articles contributed on matters of general interest.

Apart from becoming the permanent peace-time record of the Regiment's activities, it also assumed an important role in the general life of the Regiment. It became the medium of communication between the various parts and members, so that through its columns the Regimental Association could hold reunions and meetings, contributors could present items to the museum, and appeals for funds could be made, such as the Comforts Appeal while the 1st Battalion was in Malaya. More than this, it played its part in the recruiting campaign, owing to close liaison with the County newspapers. In fact, it became the central link in connecting all members of the Regiment, whether active or retired.

Lieutenant-Colonel Hunt handed over the editorship to Lieutenant-Colonel A. C. M. Urwick in 1955, who continued to edit the *Light Bob Gazette* until, on amalgamation, it became the *Light Bob*, incorporating both the *Light Bob Gazette* and the *One and All* of the Duke of Cornwall's Light Infantry. The new Regimental Magazine will continue to be produced at Taunton under Colonel Urwick's direction.

Appendix S

THE REGIMENTAL DINNER CLUB

On 20 May 1959 was held the seventy-sixth and final dinner of the Somerset Light Infantry dinner club. This dinner had been held annually ever since 1870, eighty-nine years before, with the exception of the periods during the two World Wars, during the South African War and in the year of the death of King Edward VII.

It was fitting that at this final dinner the Regiment should have as its guest Lord Lothian, the great-great-nephew of the man who had instituted the first dinner. In fact, two ancestors of Lord Lothian are closely connected with the Regiment, both bearing the name and title of 'Lord Mark Kerr'. The first was colonel of the XIIIth from December 1725 until May 1732: the second, the founder of the dinner, from February 1880 until his death in May 1900. The former, a colourful character with a campaigning and duelling record of some distinction, is possibly unfairly eclipsed by the astonishing second Lord Mark, the victor of Azimghur during the Indian Mutiny, whose subsequent activities at least served to keep the name of his regiment constantly before the authorities in Whitehall and whose 'Light Infantryness' knew no bounds.

Numbers attending the dinner have inevitably fluctuated according to the exigencies of the service, but when ninety-seven members sat down to dine at this last dinner, wearing evening dress, orders, decorations and medals, with the Attardan displayed before them, it formed a fitting climax to the long series. Although the hard core of the diners was inevitably the serving and retired Regular officers of the Regiment, many Territorial officers attended, as did some officers who served with the Regiment during the last war.

In 1946 a complementary dinner to that held in London was started in Taunton by Major-General Majendie when he

160

was Colonel of the Regiment. This has been a deservedly successful event ever since; catering for those members of the Regiment who cannot easily travel to London, it brings the Regiment annually into the County.

With the amalgamation of the Somerset Light Infantry with the Duke of Cornwall's Light Infantry, the annual dinner will in future be a combined occasion in London. The dinner in Taunton will also continue.

BIBLIOGRAPHY

The History of the Somerset Light Infantry (Prince Albert's) 1685–1914: Major-General Sir Henry Everett, K.C.M.G., C.B. Methuen and Co. Ltd, 1934.

The History of the Somerset Light Infantry (Prince Albert's) 1914–1919: Everard Wyrall. Methuen and Co. Ltd, 1927.

The History of the Somerset Light Infantry (Prince Albert's) 1919–1945: George Molesworth. Printed privately by Butler and Tanner Ltd, Frome and London, 1951.

A Journal of the Disasters in Affghanistan, 1841–2: Lady Sale. John Murray, 1843.

A Soldier's Story: A. H. Cook, edited by George Molesworth. Goodmans, Taunton, 1956.

The History of the 4th Battalion the Somerset Light Infantry: (Prince Albert's) in the Campaign in North-West Europe June 1944–May 1945: Anon. Goodmans, Taunton, undated. Issued privately.

The Story of the 7th Battalion the Somerset Light Infantry: Captain J. L. Meredith. Printed and issued privately in Germany in 1945.

Incidents with the 7th Battalion the Somerset Light Infantry in France and Germany: Anon. Printed and issued privately in Germany in 1946.

Colonel of Dragoons: Philip Woodruff. Jonathan Cape, 1951.

Way to Glory: The Life of Henry Havelock of Lucknow: J. C. Pollock. John Murray, 1957.

The Door marked Malaya: Oliver Crawford. Rupert Hart-Davis, 1958.

INDEX